D1300017

design ELEMENTS:
Form & Space

WITHDRAWN

ROCKPORT

Text and Design © 2011 by Rockport Publishers

First published in the United States of America in 2011 by Rockport Publishers, a member of Quayside Publishing Group

100 Cummings Center
Suite 406-L
Beverly, Massachusetts 01915-6101
Telephone: (978) 282-9590
Fax: (978) 283-2742
www.rockpub.com

All rights reserved. No part of this book may be reproduced in any form without written permission of the copyright owners. All images in this book have been reproduced with the knowledge and prior consent of the artists concerned, and no responsibility is accepted by producer, publisher, or printer for any infringement of copyright or otherwise, arising from the contents of this publication. Every effort has been made to ensure that credits accurately comply with information supplied. We apologize for any inaccuracies that may have occurred and will resolve inaccurate or missing information in a subsequent reprinting of the book.

10 9 8 7 6 5 4 3 2 1

ISBN-13: 978-1-59253-700-6
ISBN-10: 1-59253-700-6

Digital edition published in 2011
eISBN-13: 978-1-61058-041-0

Library of Congress Cataloging-in-Publication Data available

Design: Dennis M. Puhalla, Ph.D

Printed in China

a graphic style manual for understanding **structure** and **design**

design ELEMENTS:
Form & Space

Dennis M. Puhalla, Ph.D

contents:

1   2

701.8
PUH

3   4   5

examining form and space

Introduction

*"Non c'è niente nella vita così normale che
non possa essere fatto straordinario."*

"There is nothing in life so ordinary that
it cannot be made extraordinary."

—Italian proverb

Guided by experience, experiment, and observation, empirical knowledge is central to perception. Perception is the process by which we acquire information about the world around us using our five senses. Sight, sound, touch, smell, and taste are the ways we experience the world. From this epistemological orientation, Immanuel Kant is the foremost figure. From a Kantian philosophical tradition, it is representation that makes the object possible, rather than the object that makes the representation possible. Therefore, experiencing the world is dependent on a conceptual structure providing representational properties of experience. Reasoning connects the world we experience through structure. The rational structure of the mind reflects the rational structure of the world and the objects in it. The human mind is an active originator of experience, rather than just a passive recipient of perception. The human mind is a blank tablet; perceptual input must be processed to be recognized or it would just be noise.

The focus of *Design Elements: Form and Space* is centered on an aesthetic understanding of form in the context of ordering space. The elements of spatial organization are central to visual interpretation and perception. These elements form a visual language.

Language systems employ syntax, which govern the rules of order in which words or other elements of structure are combined to form grammatical sentences.

Language construction is also dependent upon hierarchical structuring. Implicit hierarchical structuring increases the human ability to perceive similarities and differences among things. It preserves meaning in writing, speaking, and visual representation. The basis of hierarchical structuring refers to the observed degree of contrast and similarities within each category of the mass space elements. Based upon their attributes, this results in a perceived visual hierarchy.

Principles of visual language are linked to the study of semiotics. It was de Saussure who saw language as a system within which words act as arbitrary signs.

Semiotics encompasses the theory of signs and symbolism. It expands the structure and order of language to include not only words but also assorted systems of communication. Language is any system that communicates written words, signs, symbols, images, and music. Therefore, meaning is constructed through semiotics and logical syntax represented by the formal relationships of its system of parts.

The inherent ingredients of the mass space elements—point, line, plane, and volume—generate the **syntax** of a **visual language system**. Along with the attributes of shape, size, color, and texture, they formulate the visual language structure within the boundaries of the image area. Understanding the basic premise of spatial structure and organization is critical to defining an orderly arrangement of parts.

examining form and space

Aesthetic value is a complex philosophical argument derived from human response to objects or other visual phenomena. Obviously, human response to visual phenomena is filtered through cultural surroundings and other human sensory conditions. This human response is the consequence of an assumed premise and a degree of probability relative to that premise. This response to visual stimuli amounts to an interpretation of form that applies subjective criteria, which carries emotional inferences.

Aesthetic value can be defined in objective terms by analyzing and applying a system of orderly arrangement—a visual language system. Fundamentally, the human visual condition seeks to order space and to reject chaos. There is a limit to what we can visually process. Applying the rules of simplicity and avoiding visual noise is dependent upon identifying objective visual criteria. The analysis of form and space structure is based upon the logical and rational underlying components of the mass/space elements, their physical attributes, and our explicit perceptions. Our perceptions are learned and vary according to cultural preferences rather than being inherent.

Principles of visual organization are anchored in the idea that the simplest interpretations of form and space are preferred. German psychologists developed theories on visual perception in the 1920s. These theories are manifested in Gestalt psychology, a term that means "unified whole." The theory of perceptual psychology describes how people tend to organize visual elements into groups or unified wholes when certain principles are applied. The Gestalt principles reinforce the concept that meaning is learned and constructed though perception. Thus, the Laws of Gestalt are inextricably tied to understanding form and spatial organization.

Learning to see clearly and objectively requires acute fundamental visual awareness that is not clouded by subjective inferences. What we think we see may differ from the hidden visual truth.

principles — **inspiration**

understanding — creativity

ordinary state — **extra-ordinary state**

modification — originality

manipulation — ingenuity

alteration — inventiveness

The first step in designing something extraordinary is to define the elements that make it ordinary. Thoughtful manipulation of the ordinary state of form is a contributing factor in bringing forth new images.

1

"A stone, a tree, or a fish has its own particular type of existence. The stone is static with latent perpendicular movement of its weight. The tree can expand in any direction but cannot change its position. The fish can move and take any position. Each behaves according to its specific nature. Similarly, any visible unit place on a picture-plane germinates a life of its own."

—György Kepes, *Language of Vision*

Spatial Forces

image area and the implied forces

image area and the implied forces

The image area is defined by the boundary of the picture plane, which is contained by a regular or a semiregular polygon. Typically, the common image area, also called format, is a square or rectangle.

With sides of equal length that meet at right angles, the square constitutes a regular polygon represented by a 1:1 height-to-width ratio. The square is the elemental polygon that forms the basic geometry of most proportional systems. It is the basis that determines the height-to-width ratio of a rectangle. Since the square resides in a 1:1 height-to-width ratio, it is considered to be a polygon that resides in a static state. The directional and thus visual emphasis of the height-and-width dimension remains constant.

Five specific structural forces govern the image area of the square. The implied divisions of the square and rectangle are constituted in part by three internal axes—the vertical axis, the horizontal axis, and the diagonal axis. In addition, the center point of the square is intrinsically evident. The fifth implied force is the circle residing geometrically congruent to the internal center points of the square's four sides.

The ambiguous active/passive dimension of the diagonals is dependent upon subjective interpretation. Diagonals, which move from an upper-left position to a bottom-right position, read differently from those that move from an upper-right position to a bottom-left position. This has to do with the way individuals have been taught to read. Reading from left to right or right to left influences the visual active/passive perceptual state.

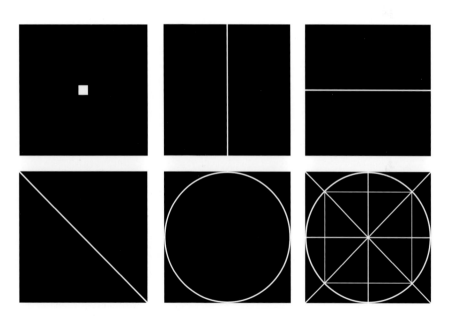

Inherent forces within the image area are visual
components that must be considered.

The square continues to generate additional
implied forces as represented with a quarter
circle, a congruent square circumscribed
within the circle, and various iterations.

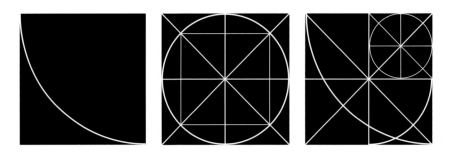

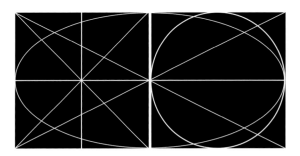

A square is the foundation of a rectangle. A rectangle
generates an implied center point, a vertical, a horizontal
and diagonals—a corner-to-corner relationship that
intersects the center point.

The center point of the square is intuitively understood.
Slight variation in the position of the center point is
easily perceived as off center.

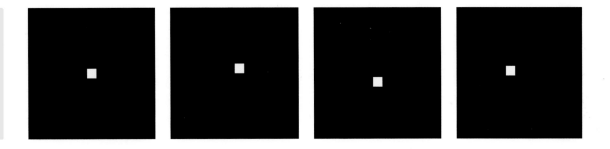

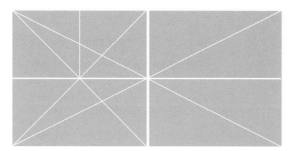

The image area of the photograph Land + Sky + Time is a rectangular composition in which the width is double the height. Notice how the horizon naturally divides the image into two equal parts. Also, the photograph is deliberately divided vertically into two equal parts—one gray tone and one sepia tone. The upper-left gray area forms two squares. The bottom-right sepia area forms two rectangles. These literal divisions of the space work in harmony with the implied forces of the square and rectangle. As a result, the divisions within the landscape suggest an orderly sequence of time in space.

Photograph: Land + Sky + Time
D. M. Puhalla

Design: Victoria Karoleff

Design: Lucas Langus

This image is a visual exploration of typographic elements to define space. Fundamentally, the square is divided into two rectangles. The major division occurs along the inherent center-vertical axis of the square, creating two rectangles. The rectangle on the left is divided into a large part and a distinct smaller part while the rectangle on the right remains an uninterrupted black. The vertical and horizontal divisions of space are composed of letterforms. As a result, the divisions are implied and less literal. These simple graphic divisions of space establish unity through similarity of parts and contrast of scale/size.

Employing a 45-degree angle, the image area of the square is divided into two parts forming implied right-angle triangles. Extending or projecting the edge of the letter *i* in bold letters forms another 45-degree angle establishing a triangle in the bottom-left corner and a five-sided polygon in the upper-right corner. In turn, the two 45-degree angles form an intersection slightly off the center point of the image area of the square. By shifting the intersection point of the two 45-degree angles off center, the division of space is less predictable, offers contrast, and is visually stimulating. The shape and visual texture of the body of text in the upper left also contrasts the rectangular body of text in the bottom-right corner.

Design: Rachel Mason

Design: Rachel Mason

The circle is intrinsically tangent to the midpoints of the square. This example integrates concentric circles, which reinforce the implied forces of the square. A dynamic interaction between the focal point of circle and the implied center point of the square is initiated by placing the circle slightly off the square's center point.

The relationship of the circle to the square may include one quarter of the circle. This example uses an implied representation of the arc of a circle to build upon the one preceding concentric circle theme.

Design: Rachel Mason

Design: Lucas Langus

The two examples define angles, which are not inherently implied in the image area. Each image employs distinct spacing between the linear elements, creating more dynamic and less predictable outcomes.

On the cover brochure for the *Thirty-Eighth International Viola Congress*, the image area is defined by a strong vertical rectangle. Internally, a set of four squares defines a larger square within the image area rectangle. With the inclusion of images, typography, symbology, color, line, and shape elements, the content drives the message. As in a musical score, the image reflects an underlying ordering system of repetition, contrasts, and surprise.

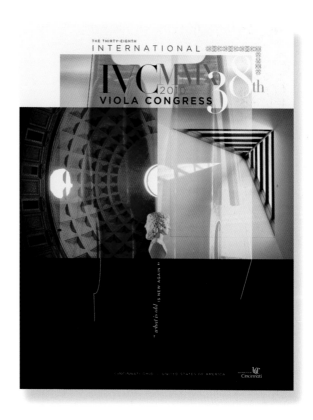

Implications

Design: Darrin Hunter

These five implied spatial forces serve as reference points and must be taken into account before displacing or dividing the surface area of the square. Literal divisions of the square that are parallel to the vertical, horizontal, and diagonal are congruent and therefore reside in concert with the implied spatial dynamics. Divisions that are at an acute or obtuse angle to the axes are in tension with the implied visual forces. Tension occurs when attracting forces are pulled in opposing directions.

2

"The real voyage of discovery consists not in seeking new landscapes but in having new eyes."

—Marcel Proust

Spatial Order

the language of form

the language of form

The **language of form** is defined by its components. These components are composed of the mass/space elements and their visible attributes, which constitute the basic **syntax/structure** of form language. The orderly arrangement among these components frames the foundation of a structured visual system. A system of parts formulates a harmonious whole. This language also constitutes a means by which objective criteria may be applied to analyze the visual elements within the image area.

Principles of spatial organization are divided into three categories. The **mass/space elements** are the foundation of spatial organization. The second defines the **attributes of the elements**. In other words, in order for the mass/space elements to have a visual presence, they must have certain innate characteristics. The third category establishes a structure, which addresses the **perceptual framework** of visual processing.

The three categories that comprise the principles of spatial organization also establish the language of visual form. Additionally, the language of visual form provides the basis for objective criteria to analyze the strengths and weaknesses of graphic organization.

ELEMENTS   **ATTRIBUTES**   **PERCEIVED ATTRIBUTES & ELEMENTS**

		hierarchy
		alignment, position, projection, trajectory, orientation, direction, proximity, rotation
		sequence/interval
		transitions, connections, convergence, terminations
		number/density
point	color	axis
line	size	balance
plane	shape	symmetry
volume	texture	tension
		rhythm
		closure
		fluctuation
		afterimage
		grouping
		focal point

Mass | Space Elements

form language components

elements: point—line—plane—volume

The mass/space elements are the graphic components used to organize an image area. The elements progress from simple to complex. That is, a point generates a line. Lines in turn generate planes and volume within the image area. These components represent the most ordinary and fundamental method of organizing or dividing space. All graphic devices employed in a composition can be extracted and transformed into these essential mass/space elements.

Undeniably, the mass/space elements are familiar, commonplace, typical, and fundamentally simplistic. However, an explanation of these elements is necessary to clarify meaning in a visual context. The harmonious relationship of parts that form a composition is dependent upon the order, interaction, and function of these elements.

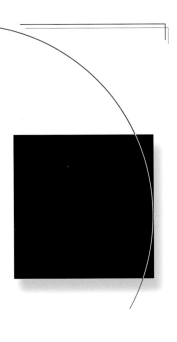

Point, line, plane, and volume are basic elements of spatial division.

Point

A point is the simplest component of the elements. Mathematically, a point has no dimension. Visually, a point is represented graphically as a dot or mark. Comparatively, a point is small in relationship to the image area surface.

A point placed within the image area defines a position in space. As illustrated earlier, the implied center of the square is readily apparent to the human eye. Therefore, a dot placed slightly off center will appear misplaced or inaccurately positioned. Generally, the dot is best positioned decisively on center or decisively off center. Points reside in harmony or in dissonance with the implied forces of a square so a point positioned on center is in harmony within the square. When the point is positioned on center, the surrounding area is equally divided, but it is a predictable geometric location that is visually static. Whereas a point positioned off center is visually dynamic and activates newly formed implied proportional divisions of the space. Understanding the proportional divisions of the space establishes an objective rationale for a point's location.

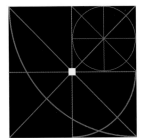 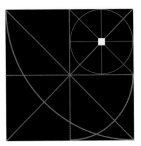 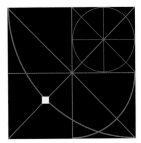 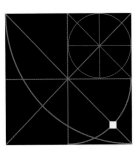

Decisive positioning of a point in relation to the implied forces creates a visual rationale for its location.
As with all of the elements, points establish a static or dynamic interaction of parts within the whole.

Placement of the word *contents* affords the opportunity for the letter *o* to function as a dot in space. In addition, the *o* dot serves to interact with the half circle shape, which is positioned along the left edge of the composition. Imagine a straight line running between the *o* dot and the half circle. The edge of the implied line would be tangent to the left edge of the *o* dot and the right edge of the half circle. The *o* dot is also tangent to the edge of the diagonal of the image area square. The deliberate and thoughtful positioning between the dot and half circle activates a visual dynamic in the composition.

Design: Kristin Cullen

Design: Michael Bierut and Armin Vit
Pentagram Design, New York

The original symbol was designed by the artist Martyl in 1947.

Placing a number of points that are close in proximity and similar in size and shape creates an implied line. The points along an implied path are used to create eye movement within the image area of the composition.

This simple arrangement of points and lines is easily recognized as a clock. The dots are uniformly sequenced to imply movement from one point to the next. The starkness of the image reflects the intent of the message. Redesign of the Doomsday Clock symbol for the *Bulletin of the Atomic Scientists*.

Line

A line is characterized as the path of a moving point. As such, a point transitions and transforms figuratively into line. According to Euclidean geometry, a line continues infinitely in length and has no width or height. As a visual graphic representation, a line segment is a stroke straight or curved that is long in proportion to its width. Lines may be categorized as straight, regularly curved, and compound curved.

A **regular curved** line emerging from the circumference of the circle is an arc. It reaches its apex at the center point of the arc, and then it ascends and peaks at the center. From the center point, the line changes direction and descends to its endpoint.

An **increasing curve** is generated by no more than one fourth of an ellipse or less. As a point moves along the path of an ellipse, the line transitions from a tight radius to one that successively increases. As the radius increases, it encompasses a larger surface area.

Variable curves are generated by any number of regular and/or increasing curves that are linked together. They form a smooth uninterrupted line edge, or the edge may turn direction sharply and create a break point.

Lines positioned parallel, perpendicular, or diagonally reside in harmony with the implied forces of the image area. Along these axes, positioning is stable and explicit.

However, lines positioned at acute or obtuse angles are not an ordinary visual expectation, but they can appear visually dynamic. Neither arrangement is better than the other. Visual sensitivity to line positioning and spatial division are significantly important to communicating a visual message. It is also important to note that the relationship of lines can be perceived as friendly, compatible, and passive. Angular linear relationships may be perceived as assertive and aggressively active.

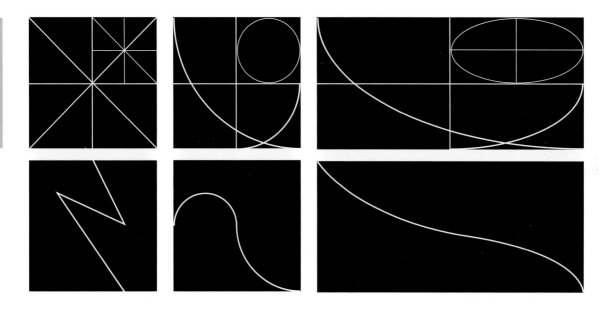

Line elements are formed from regular geometry. Various configurations of lines generate angular relationships and curved line segments. Regular curves are directly related to the arc of a circle and increasing curves are no more than one fourth of an ellipse. Variable curved lines are the product of numerous regular and variable curves linked together.

Curved lines are fluid and perceived as relatively passive. Perhaps this is due to our associations with nature and the human body. Even so, curves employ directional emphasis along a path that acts to engage or reject areas within a composition. Concave lines engage an area of space while convex lines push into the surface area of the composition.

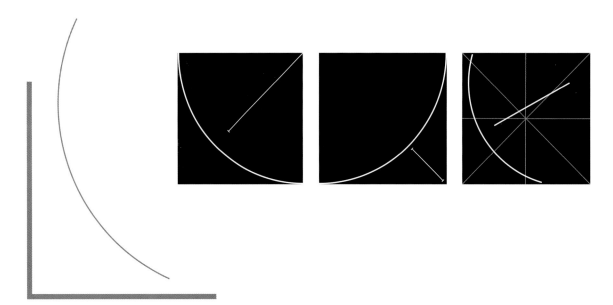

Lines residing congruent to the implied forces are in harmony with those forces. Lines residing at acute or obtuse angles to the implied forces are in tension with those forces. The convex and concave direction of the arc of a circle also creates a visual emphasis. The concave side engages the surface area within it while the convex side of the arc repels corners and edges.

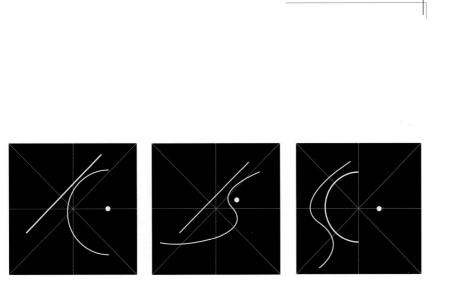

A regular curved arc pushes the straight line outward and pulls the point inward. A similar thing happens with the variable curved line. In the previous illustration, the variable curve engages the regular curve along the top edge. Toward the bottom, the two curves form a bottleneck as they push outward. If projected, the point would follow a path that would divide the two curves at their apex. The apex is the point of a curve that transitions from ascent to descent.

In this photograph, two concentric circles are positioned at the midpoint of the right vertical edge of the composition. As a result, the composition is equally divided in half—top and bottom. To create visual interest, the circle's center point occurs outside the image area. The concave portion of the circles pulls the right edge of the composition inward. The structural elements of the valve function as straight and regular curved lines.

Photograph: Kristin Cullen

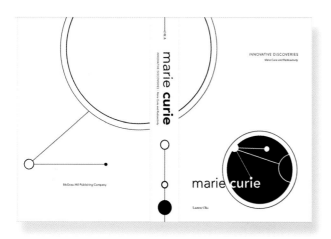

Dots and circles are the primary visual components in this book cover layout. Intersecting lines and points along the vertical axis engage the primary circle. Angular linear relationships provide contrast and assist movement of the eye across the image area.

Design: Lauren Oka

By carefully observing type in the environment, a letter and number in an oval dot are the focal point of this composition, located on the vertical center of the image. The white line along the top of the image is approximately the same thickness as the black line above it. The irregular shape within the top edge of the white line acts as a secondary point of interest. As a result, this simple image generates eye movement and has a strong visual impact.

Photograph: Kristin Cullen

Consistent control of the line and dot elements is the basis of the letter characters AIFJR.

Design: Victoria Karoleff

Design: Laura Frycek

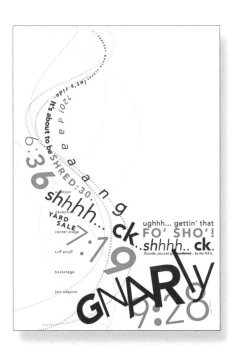

Design: Lauren Oka

Type follows the path of straight lines, which are at right angles. Regular curved arcs and variable curved lines are defined with typography, as well. To a lesser extent, various angular type lines are employed to provide contrast to the compositional structure.

The primary structure of this type study consists of variable curves that are congruently engaged. Additional variable curves act in a contrasting fashion, as they appear to push against the congruent line paths.

Photograph: Kristin Cullen

The vertical railing and the space between the rails form lines. The sequence of lines that appear behind the rails increase in their width as they move from left to right. Circular dots serve as containers for the letterforms. The type interrupted by the vertical railing also moves left to right. Together, line, dots, and type create left to right eye movement in the composition.

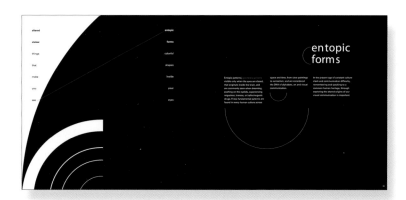

Design: Lynda Lucas

Entopic is Greek for "within the eye." Entopic patterns are geometric patterns that become visible only when the eyes are closed. They originate inside the brain and are commonly seen when dreaming, pushing on the eyelids, experiencing migraines, trances, or hallucinogenic drugs. These fundamental patterns are found in every human culture across space and time, from cave paintings to surrealism, and are considered the DNA of alphabets, art, and visual communication.

These patterns are directly associated with dots, angular lines, parallel lines, concentric circles, grids, and filigrees. This information graphic is a two-page example of multiple pages. "Information Graphics" provides a visual explanation of simple entopic forms and how they were used and interpreted.

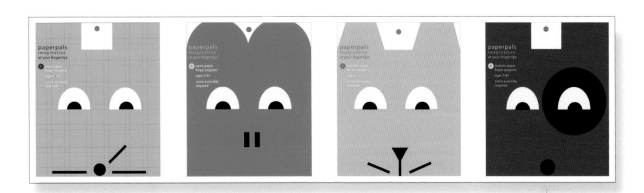

Design: Laura Frycek

These images represent a method of integrating line and shape elements to represent figures in a concise and meaningful way. Circular shapes and line are the focal elements employed in this paper toy of animal likenesses. The visual scale of line and shape remains consistent throughout each image.

Plane

A two-dimensional surface area generated by connected straight and/or curved lines creates a plane. A plane can take the form of any shape and resides on the picture plane. Regular or semiregular polygons formulate a plane as well as a closed curved configured circle and ellipse. Each shape is innately structured with implied visual forces as established in the square.

The square, circle, and triangle are rudimentary shapes that form planes. They tend to appear in a parallel position in relation to the surface of the image area. They also serve to generate a multitude of additional regular and irregular configurations.

Design: Michael Bierut and Jennifer Kinon
Pentagram Design, New York

Letterforms are specifically integrated into rectangular shapes for Saks Fifth Avenue "Think About It" campaign.

Design: Lippincott, New York

Vale Mining identity, Wana identity, and GLAAD media-award brochures, are examples that focus on the variable curve as a primary visual element incorporating restrained geometric shapes.

Wana is Morocco's global telecom company offering fixed line, mobile, and Internet services. Every aspect of the brand design was carefully and deliberately crafted. The Wana symbol, a dynamic star, references the Moroccan flag and connects with the Moroccan spirit.

Volume

The amount of three-dimensional space a shape or object occupies may seem irrelevant here since a two-dimensional graphic space has no depth. However, creating depth illusion is an important factor that contributes to visual stimulation. Understanding the visual power of volume is particularly important for a variety of graphic design applications. In addition to print media, other graphic applications include packaging, time-based media—motion graphics, websites, environmental graphics, and wayfinding systems. All of these applications must consider three-dimensional use of volume and space. Even some color systems are organized in a three-dimensional color space.

Volume portrayed on a two-dimensional surface is perceived through cognitive processing. On a two-dimensional surface, the visual characteristics of objects influence our perceptual depth cues. Size, shape, color, layering, transparency, overlapping, and angles are commonly used to communicate depth on a two-dimensional surface.

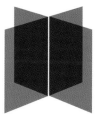

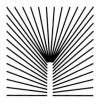

Planar and angular relationships on a two-dimensional picture plane create the illusion of a three-dimensional space. There are three types of volume—a clearly circumscribed mass, a negative volume, and a virtual volume. Understanding the nature of the three types helps the designer control variables and avoids visual confusion.

A clearly circumscribed mass is a convex solid. These objects have no concave components. Consequently, these objects define a positive surface area. The Platonic and Archimedean solids are examples of a continuous convex surface.

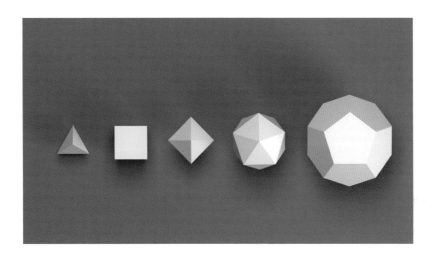

Illustration: Matt Puhalla

The five Platonic solids are a clearly circumscribed mass defined by regular polygons, which are formed by one shape type. A clearly circumscribed mass is a convex solid. These objects have no concave components. Consequently, these objects define a positive surface area. The Platonic and Archimedean solids are examples of a continuous convex surface. These solids are regular convex polyhedra that are defined by one type regular polygon—square, equilateral triangle, pentagon. They are composed of the tetrahedron, hexahedron, octahedron, dodecahedron, and the icosahedrons. The Archimedean solids are semiregular convex polyhedra composed of two or more types of regular polygons. There are thirteen Archimedean solids.

A negative volume consists of a concavity or a void. A solid with a surface impression defines a negative area. Cups and bowls are objects that define a negative space.

Points, lines, and planes in space define a virtual volume. For example, a table with a top and four legs occupies an area of space. Yet the space below the top surface and between the four legs is empty. The empty space is considered to be a part of the whole volume the table defines.

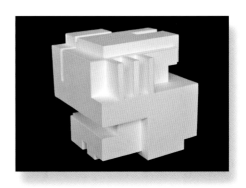

Design: Branden Francis

Planes, edges, and points define the total surface area of a cube. Since the cube is implied, the object is indicative of a virtual volume.

Design: Matt Puhalla
MNML Design, Chicago

These tea vessels are examples of negative volume. Each component fits within the other.

Design: Matt Puhalla

Aspects of a virtual volume are portrayed in this slat chair. Lines and planes define a mass area in space. Notice how the area of the seat and back are defined by implied surfaces along the contour. The metal tubular frame acts as a line contoured along straight and curved paths. This technique gives the chair a light and airy feeling.

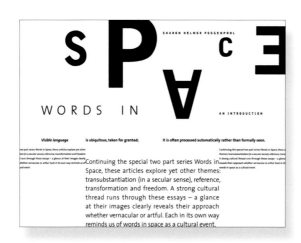

Design: Kristin Cullen

This image is a detail of an interior spread for the design journal, *Visible Language*. Words inhabit space from all directions, including the gutter, without altering authors' words or altering the text. The design takes full advantage of book space by using the parts of a book that are typically unused. Changes in size and orientation communicate spatial positioning and volume.

The Light Years poster for the Architectural League of New York employs the use of layering and transparency, producing the illusion of light, space, and volume.

Design: Michael Bierut
Pentagram Design, New York

The goal of this tactile puzzle is intended to get the viewer intimately involved with the design. Touching is as important as looking. Note the use of geometric typographical elements that differ in their depth dimension.

Design: Lindsay Quinter

Design: Chermayeff & Geismar, New York

The office tower at 9 West 57th Street in New York City is a giant ski-slope of a building designed by Skidmore, Owings & Merrill. This huge, red *9* sits on the sidewalk on city property and marks the building's main entrance. It has become a dynamic New York landmark. The volume of the number in the environment makes a powerful visual statement.

For over thirty years, this dimensional letter concept and related dimensional station call letters have served as a theme to identify WGBH, the Boston-based PBS television station. The visual articulation of volume provides a dimensional quality appropriate for motion graphics and print media.

Design: Chermayeff & Geismar, New York

Design: Chermayeff & Geismar, New York

The Chase logo used abstract geometric elements for its identification. Radical for its time, the Chase symbol has survived a number of subsequent mergers and has become one of the world's most recognizable trademarks. In this example, the geometry of the two-dimensional image is transformed into three-dimensional planes, which allows the form to remain a single color consistent with the two-dimensional logo.

The AMESCO metal mark is another example of a three-dimensional transformation from a two-dimensional mark. The company represents five generations of metal and steel traders. The symbol incorporates three capital *A*'s. Additionally, the symbol suggests strength, structure, and building.

Design: Chermayeff & Geismar, New York

Packaging by its very nature is volumetric. These packages of Liz Claiborne for men incorporate squares and rectangles in three-dimensional visual units.

Mass | Space Attributes

form language features

attributes: shape—color—texture—size

The mass/space elements are described by their visual and physical attributes and distinguishing features. The attributes are characterized by shape, color, texture, and size. It is the attribute of an object that signals identity and gives meaning to form. Multiple shapes, colors, textures, and sizes are found in nature and the built environment.

Shape

Shapes are self-contained outlines or surfaces that are defined by regular polygons or variable-sided polygons and closed curved configurations. Shapes innately create visual stimuli that incorporate the attributes of color, texture, and size/scale. Shapes, like planes, are parallel to the image area that rest flat on a two-dimensional surface but may also have a 3-D appearance. Even shapes with the most complex configuration are usually derivatives of simple basic geometry.

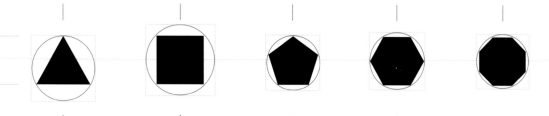

The equilateral triangle, square, pentagon, hexagon, and octagon are regular polygons having equal sides and angles. Each polygon in the illustration shares the same centered vertical dimension, but the polygons do not appear to be similar in size. When the circumference of a circle is centered on a regular polygon, the points of the polygon are always tangent to the circle.

This illustration shows the construction of a pentagon as it relates to a circle. The first six steps are necessary to determine the length of the side of the pentagon. Once that is determined, the line is placed tangent to the inside of the circle's circumference. As shown, the five-pointed star is derived from the five points of the pentagon. The last drawing shows a 180-degree rotation of two pentagons that form a ten-sided regular polygon.

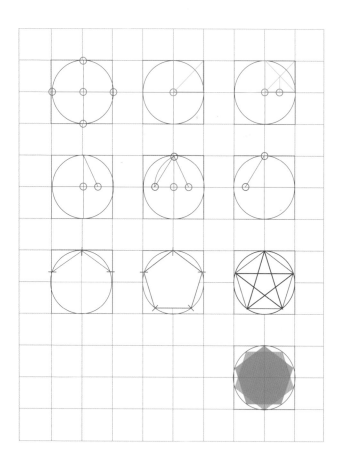

55

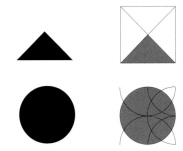

Regular polygons form tile tessellations consisting of two or more types of regular polygons. In this example, the square and equilateral triangle define the tessellation.

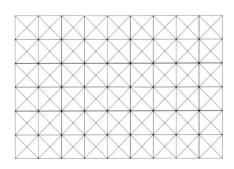

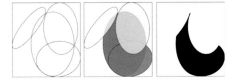

Organic shapes with an irregular contour are derived from basic polygons, circles, and ellipses. The underlying geometric shapes have axes, which give directional emphasis to the organic form.

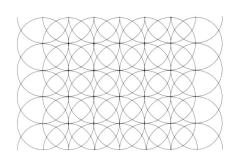

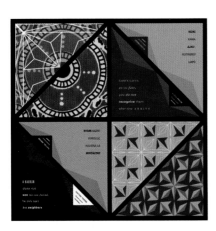

Design: Jen Vitello

This illustrates how a complex form is derived from a simple triangle and circle, which allows for exploration and variation. Using a square that could fold and connect into a much larger, more complex form is the basis for this information graphic. The possibilities of creating flat and dimensional structures offer many alternatives. The design of the spreads fits within the square grid. The form was designed to separate content and provide order to the incorporation of photography, patterns, and other elements. Consideration is given to each spread individually as well as each part of the whole piece. The intent was to create an interactive piece so the viewer could fold it in multiple ways and view different spreads next to each other.

These images utilize tessellations derived from closed curved shapes. The organic shapes suggest a structure that is indicative of continued growth and expansion.

The Tennessee Aquarium is focused on the abundant freshwater fish, bird, and animal life of Tennessee's rivers and their tributaries. This Lisbon Aquarium is dedicated to the sea life of the open ocean and houses a vast array of marine creatures.

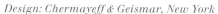

Design: Chermayeff & Geismar, New York

The strong triangular red/white shape in the 2006 DAAP Works poster is a segment of a five pointed star. The angles that form this triangle are echoed in the structural design of the composition. It also serves as a visual cue leading the eye to the text-based content of the poster. Note how the white shape directs the viewer to the word, "daapWorks."

The composition also incorporates spatial depth through the use of layering and perspective. Circular/dot shapes derived from the typeface Dr. No by Ian Anderson provide contrast to the sharp angles.

Design: Kristin Cullen

The combination of geometric and organic shapes function as a harmonious whole in this nonprofit finance logo. The angular structure on the left and right sides suggest a two- and three-dimensional spatial configuration.

The geometric logo for Argentinian broadcaster Artear was inspired by the Argentinian sun. It is made of interlocking elements around an open center. The logo is also similar to the flag of Argentina.

Design: Steff Geissbuhler, C&G Partners, New York

Founded as Universal Press Syndicate, Andrews McMeel Universal diversified and began publishing humor, self-improvement books, syndicated columns, and cartoons. The mark uses the letter *U* for Universal. Two added eyes to the letter *U* make it into a face. The letter *U* is defined by two rectangles and a segment of an arc of a circle.

Alhurra (Arabic for "the free one") is an Arabic-language satellite TV network. The mark is defined by three lines of color and two linear negative spaces. The linear elements function as a whole to define the overall shape.

This system of symbol signs was designed for use in airports, transportation hubs, and at large international events. They were produced through a collaboration between the American Institute of Graphic Artists (AIGA) and the U.S. Department of Transportation (DOT). The symbol signs are an example of how public-minded designers can address a universal communication need. AIGA appointed a committee of five leading designers of environmental graphics, who evaluated the symbols and made recommendations for adapting or redesigning them. Based on their conclusions, a team of AIGA member designers produced the symbols.

These symbols are deliberately constrained and consistent in geometric shape relationships. Note the similarity of circle shapes, line weights, and angles. The symbols are intended to be legible in small or large format.

Design: AIGA Symbol Sign Commission

Color

Points, lines, and planes also have a color attribute. It encompasses three properties or dimensions—hue, value, and chroma.

Hue is the generic family name of color. For example, a blue hue is the root of all blues that appear light, dark, bright, or dull.

The **value** of a color is characterized by its relative lightness or darkness. A color appears light if it is placed in the context of a color that is darker. Generally, light colors that appear to have white in them are called **tints**, while colors that appear to have black in them are called **shades**.

The third property of color is **chroma**, or purity. Chroma has two distinguishing characteristics—saturation and brightness. Colors at full saturation cannot be made more colorful. Desaturated colors appear to have a gray tone. A tone is a derivative of a fully saturated color that has been modified with gray. As colors appear grayer they become dull or less bright. The terms brightness and intensity are often used interchangeably. However, consider the possibility that brightness is dependant upon our perception of a color while intensity is dependent upon the wavelength of a color. One deals with cognitive processing and the other deals with scientifically measured calculations.

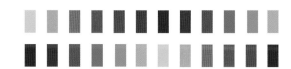

HUE
Hue is a property of color that represents the generic names of family groups within the visible spectrum.

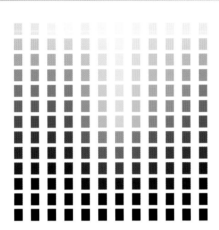

VALUE

Each hue is represented in different light to dark values along the vertical column. These modified colors are referred to as tints (with white) and shades (with black).

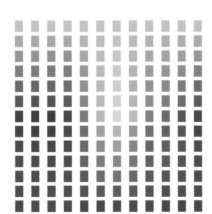

HUE and CHROMA—SATURATION

Each vertical band of color is a derivative of one hue family that has been modified with a light gray at the top of the illustration and a darker gray at the bottom. These modified colors are referred to as tones.

VALUE and SATURATION

One red-orange hue is represented in a different value within each vertical column. Along each horizontal row, the color is the same in value but it contrasts in saturation, or chroma. The same hue is represented in visually uniform units of contrast in chroma. As the saturation changes in tone, the brightness changes from bright to dull.

Design: Chermayeff & Geismar, New York

Fully saturated primary and secondary colors form the palette for these examples. No alterations have been made to modify the value or saturation of each hue.

The colors in the NBC peacock progress in an orderly sequence derived from the visible spectrum. The peacock has since become one of the world's most highly recognized trademarks.

The International Tchaikovsky Competition graphic identity system encompasses a color structure that includes two primary colors—blue and red. The secondary colors—green, orange, and purple are also included. The visual hierarchy of the red and orange dominate as they alternate between the less dominant blue, green, and purple.

Drawing on the dynamism and beauty of classical performance, this symbol elegantly suggests a number of musical associations: the five lines on a staff, the curves in a clef, the radiation of sound waves, and the lyrical flow of music.

Design: Chermayeff & Geismar, New York

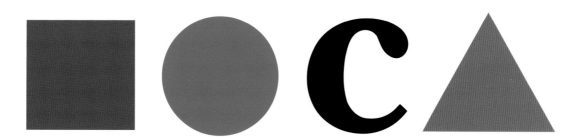

Design: Chermayeff & Geismar, New York

The Museum of Contemporary Art, Los Angeles, is an institution known for its playful and memorable identity. It's made up of the three most basic geometric forms of contemporary art—the square, the circle, and the triangle. Keeping with the simplicity of form, fully saturated primary and secondary colors are employed. They evoke contemporary art and design by pushing the boundaries of legibility.

Texture

Not only does the surface appearance of points, lines, and planes have color, they also assume texture. Controlling the variables of size, repetition, density, value, and shape can make a flat surface look dimensional, while texture on a three-dimensional surface elicits a tactile experience.

Texture is an attribute of form that is literal in a three-dimensional object and nonliteral in a two-dimensional representation. Textures are the visual and/or tactile quality of a surface.

Patterns may be perceived as texture if the units are small enough. A pattern is a graphic device that employs regular unit repetition. Once the scale of the unit forming a pattern is visually distinctive, it ceases to be a texture.

The physical structural characteristics of textures are given to a material in relation to size, shape, position, and proportion. They appear to be interwoven and derived from patterns, tessellations, or interlaced organic shapes. Generally, high-density regular or irregular units form textures.

Like color, texture assists perception and memory functions because it provides visual and tactile feedback, which affect the way, an image or object is understood and interpreted.

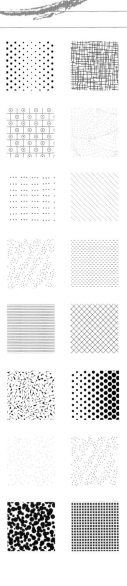

Textures in this example are created through lines and dots that vary in density.

Design: Michael Bierut and Joe Marianek
Pentagram, New York

Variations of textured surface are applied to the logo for the Museum of Arts and Design (MAD). Iterations of each logo evoke a particular visual characteristic and emotional response related to its color and texture. The texture and color content establish a purposeful context, which gives the logo meaning .

The density of the dots forms a light-to-dark texture that functions as a surface background in this Universe information booklet. In the following image, the larger white dots maintain their identity and define concentric circles. As the dots decrease in size they become dense, creating the appearance of linear textural elements. Controlling the density, color, and size, dots form textures that define a background surface—circles, chevrons, and lines.

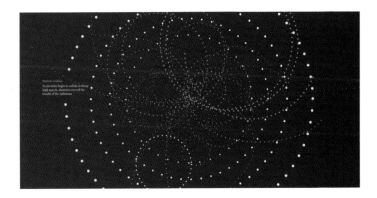

Design: Christina Cahalene

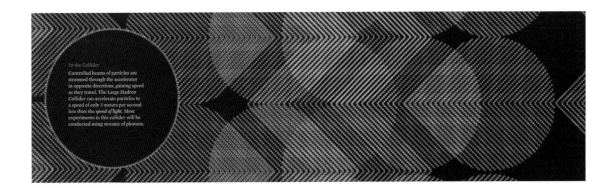

This image relies on contrast of texture, color, and size relationships. The organic configuration of grass communicates a visual textural field against the stark blue sky. In order to show differences, the basic geometric shapes of the house reinforce the comparison of opposite elements—organic and geometric; smooth and coarse.

Photograph: D. M. Puhalla

These are exquisite examples of textures that define objects and letterforms.
The illustrator captures the essence of a word in a specific context.

Illustrations: Yulia Brodskaya
Brodskaya Illustrations, United Kingdom

Size

As textures are dependent upon the density of small units, size or scale is a critical consideration. The size of objects is dependent upon several variables. Size depends upon context. Point, line, planes, shapes, color, value, texture, and position are factors that control the appearance of size.

In order for a point to appear as a point/dot, it must be placed in a context that makes it appear small. Otherwise, the point or dot becomes a shape. The length and width of lines provide visual spatial cues. On a picture surface, large shapes appear closer than smaller lines; thick lines appear closer than thinner lines.

A progressive sequence from small to large has the potential to signify or imply movement. Typically, no contrast in the size relationship of objects creates a static image having no visual directional movement.

Color and value play a significant role in the appearance of size relationships. Light, bright colors tend to make objects appear larger, while dark, dull objects tend to appear smaller.

The attribute of size may also give an object weight. On a two-dimensional surface, weight is a nonliteral representation of form: It is perceived. The visual characteristic of size relationships makes objects appear light or heavy. Larger objects tend to weigh more than smaller ones.

However, the weight of an object is dependent upon additional factors. Generally, darker objects appear heavier than lighter objects. Perhaps this visual phenomenon may be the result of our perceptual experiences in the context of our environment.

Consider the Sun shining on objects below, creating a light-to-dark gradation from top to bottom. The bottom of that object is dark, as it is shielded from light above; the gravitational pull of that object gives it weight and anchors it to the ground below. The visual feedback suggests a heavy feel at the bottom.

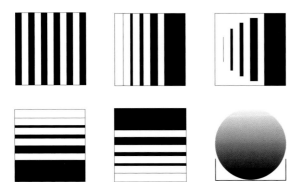

Size affects spatial and directional movement. Without contrast in size, linear elements appear static. A sequential variation in the width or length of a line provides eye movement and spatial depth.

The motion of sound waves is implied when sequential changes in size are applied.

The dots in the center of the square are all the same size. Changes in color contrast make them appear different in scale.

The size of objects suggests the illusion of weight. The ordinary orientation of weight is at the bottom. When the weight is positioned at the top, the image may appear top heavy. Since light normally comes from the top, the bottom of an image is in shade and shadow that gives the object a weighted bottom. Both size and color affect weight.

The square format in these images is the same size. Note the change in appearance of each square. Squares with vertical divisions appear as vertical rectangles while squares divided horizontally appear as wide rectangles. This vertical and horizontal visual effect also depends on the number of units employed within the square.

Design: Michael Bierut, Pentagram, New York

The Architectural League of New York changes location in the city. Announcing the change of address, typographic contrast in scale, weight, and direction conveys a message of spatial movement. The space in this example changes in depth given the changes in size and light/dark relationships. Large, bold, black type advances forward while the smaller type with a lighter gray value resides deep in space.

Mass | Space Elements and Attributes Perceived

Perceptual Structure

How we perceive and process the elements and their attributes are significant factors that contribute to aesthetic value. Achieving compositional harmony is about seeing and perceiving the parts that define the whole.

Seeing is more than looking. Learning to see is a process based upon acquired knowledge. We analyze and interpret visual images in a context. What is seen emanates from the interaction of discreet parts within the context of the whole. Truly seeing the elements described by their attributes requires freeing our vision from subjective thinking and blinded sensibilities. Seeing with clarity requires objectivity and thoughtful visual perception.

Creating a visually dynamic composition is dependent upon many factors. Conscientious awareness of how the elements and attributes within a structure interact is a fundamental factor that influences visual perception. Theories of visual perception are grounded in **Gestalt Principles**—a psychological term meaning "unified whole." Understanding these principles provides a perceptual structure and a rational explanation for organizing form and space.

In visual design and spatial organization, the Gestalt Laws that innately influence visual order are symmetry, proximity, similarity, closure, and figure–ground (Law of Prägnanz). Additionally, it is important to recognize other terms that clarify Gestalt Principles and assist in the analysis of compositional organization. These terms constitute the intrinsic properties of a visual system. Intrinsic properties include axis, alignment, grouping, connections, terminations, convergence, number, sequence, rotation, position, orientation, balance, proportion, hierarchy, focal point, weight, tension, rhythm, fluctuation, and afterimage.

The intrinsic visible properties may also serve as a checklist establishing objective criteria for analyzing compositional order. Attaining a coherent visual language is dependent upon a logical relationship of the parts that form the whole.

The order of the elements, along with their visual attributes, affects visual interpretation and reaction to the images. While the elements and attributes are visually represented as a literal function, perceptions of how they interact are conditional. Some are literal; others function as a nonliteral representation, and some are reciprocal. For example, axis, alignment, and position are literal properties that have a factual visual representation in a composition.

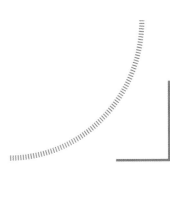

Weight, tension, and rhythm are nonliteral. The visual representation of these properties is figurative or metaphorical. In a two-dimensional space, as presented earlier, weight is an expression of a set of conditions that makes an object appear to be heavy or light. Therefore, weight is a nonliteral, intrinsic property.

When a mutual action occurs between two elements, it has a reciprocal function. The Gestalt Principle of figure and ground reversal functions as a reciprocal arrangement of parts. The figure/ground phenomenon occurs when an object appears to be visually conspicuous (figure) while the other appears secondary (ground). The ground serves as a space upon which a figure resides. When the figure becomes the ground and the ground becomes the figure, both objects mutually support each other.

Structuring form is a complex undertaking and understanding the power of perceptual functions is useful for organizing visual components. In order to analyze an image or composition objectively, rather than subjectively, the viewer must understand the way the elements, attributes, and perceptual structure function as a whole. These three categories are the components that form a dynamic, coherent, and substantive visual language system.

One of the most intriguing and visually stimulating components of perceptual structure is closure. According to Gestalt psychology, closure is a visual phenomenon that occurs when shapes are not entirely or literally connected. If the proximity of points or line endings is controlled and positioned appropriately, the image will imply a connection.

This visual phenomenon intensifies the white areas that are not joined. The closure affect is not only recognizable in regular shapes, such as squares, circles, and triangles, it is also found in pictograms, logos, ligatures, and other forms of graphic represen-tation. Closure and other visual intrinsic properties do not happen in a vacuum. They function in conjunction with one another simultaneously. Closure, for example, depends upon similarity, position, proximity, and cognition.

The perceptual function of closure occurs by reducing the graphic representation of familiar forms to essential minimal elements. Efficient use of point, line, and shape allows the eye to connect point and line trajectories. Closure intensifies the activity of the negative area, allowing the viewer to be actively involved with forming the shape of the image.

perceptual structure

literal

hierarchy   transitions
focal point   connections
                   convergence
                   terminations

axis
—visual, geometric

number/density
sequence/interval

proximity
Gestalt Law of Proximity—spatial proximity of elements are perceived as a totality

position
alignment, rotation, projection, trajectory orientation

mass/space elements and attributes perceived

nonliteral

after image + simultaneous contrast
tension
weight + balance

reciprocal

GESTALT LAW OF FIGURE/GROUND
positive + negative

closure
Gestalt Law of Closure—a perceived sensation, completing a disconnected figure

similarity/grouping
Gestalt Law of Similarity—similar elements and attributes grouped into collective entities

continuity
Gestalt Law of Continuity—perceived continuing visual patterns

The perceptual function of closure defines a square, circle, and triangle. The affect of closure produces a striking visual phenomenon. When corners are not connected, perceptual functions produce a visual glow whiter than the page itself. The shapes defined by a series of points appear whiter than the surface they rest upon. The same phenomenon occurs when the trajectory of line endings form a predictable path.

fighter plane
Design: Joseph Howell

hummingbird mark
Design: Lucas Langus

sailfish mark
Design: Lauren Oka

egret mark
Design: Laura Frycek

The explicit forms in these images are defined by integrating the principle of closure. Note that the trajectory of line or point endings align with neighboring edges to form the shape. The proximity of the point and line endings is a critical factor that links the interrupted parts. With too much interrupted space, the image would not hold together. Within each image, similar line weights, shapes, and curves form a unified whole. Each animal figure communicates the essence of its natural state.

Design Elements: **Form & Space**

Design: Jesse Reed

The edges of the top and bottom ellipse that form the 35-mm film canister are close enough in proximity to allow the eye to connect the points. The black color and shape of the film offer a vivid contrast to the implied cylinder. The black color of the film is also indicative of the character of the film itself. This image was used for a photography show poster titled, "We Still Use Film."

The Peace Corps image is a linear representation of closure. There are fifty lines (twenty-five black strokes, not including the solid olive branch, and twenty-five white spaces) to represent the fifty United States, in which the Peace Corps was founded and remains based. The line weight changes progressively, creating a dark-to-light value field for the white dove of peace. The shapes that form the dove also share a similarity in curved form.

Design: Jesse Reed

Design: Steff Geissbuhler
C&G Partners, New York

The identity of the Voice of America incorporates the closure affect and figure–ground reversal. In addition, the mark turns the *V* and *A* into inverted triangles to suggest the ability to project in many directions at once.

An event poster with the speaker's name transforming from barely recognizable to a literal use of letterforms. Even though portions of the letterforms are left out, note the speaker's name becomes readable in the fourth horizontal line of type.

Design: Mia Pizzuto

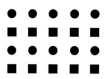

2

Similar shapes group to form a horizontal line of circles and squares.

Another component of perceptual structure is a Gestalt principle called similarity/grouping. Perceptually, elements will be grouped if they are similar to each other.

Similarity and **grouping** is dependent upon position, proximity, structure, size, shape, texture, and color. When these characteristics of form correspond to each other, it is likely the elements will be visually linked together.

Contrasting shapes are grouped according to similarity in color and shape to form a horizontal line. Color is such a powerful attribute that it makes it possible to group contrasting shapes along an angular path.

But, these elements have an innate visual hierarchy. Undeniably, a sequence of squares will group together if they are placed in close proximity and appear the same in color and size, but they will not group with a set of circles that are the same color and size. However, color is a powerful visual attribute. Different shapes can be grouped if color is employed thoughtfully.

Similarity in a composition is an essential ingredient. It is the glue that holds parts together as a harmonious whole. Similarity may contribute to eye movement from one point to another.

 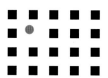

An image composed of uniform squares in a regular sequence produces a static field. Too much similarity in size, shape, orientation, and position is visually predictable. This type of configuration enables the squares to visually group and form a field or ground.

A word of caution—too much similarity will diminish eye movement and cause a composition to become static. Contrast in size, shape, or color is a necessity. On the flip side, too much contrast creates chaos. A visually dynamic composition establishes a balance between similar and contrasting elements.

In the field of static uniform squares, one red circle becomes a focal point and creates eye movement. The circular shape and position within the field of squares offers decisive visual contrast.

Photographs: Jane Park

A regular repetition of austere columns in light and shadow in this photograph sets the stage for a contrasting element. The strategic placement of a bench and bicycle in the foreground encourages eye movement and visual interest within the dimensional space.

3

"A thimbleful of red is redder than a bucketful."

—Henri Matisse

Design Elements: **Form & Space**

Color Structure

The study of color represents an array of theories dating back to Plato's *Timaeus*. Spanning centuries, scientists, astronomers, mathematicians, architects, philosophers, psychologists, physicists, chemists, engineers, and painters have contributed theoretical color models. The chronology of color theory demonstrates varying definitions, methods, and organizational strategies. Most of these systems of color organization share a common classification. Color is defined by its properties in a three-dimensional space—hue, value, and chroma.

Generally, color models are an orderly system formed by a set of primary colors in the visible spectrum. Two types of color models are classified as subtractive and additive.

Additive models result from light emitted from a color source. Subtractive models are the result of light reflected from a surface. The two most common additive and subtractive models are the RGB model (red, green, blue) and the CMYK model (cyan-magenta-yellow-black).

RGB is an additive color space. In this model merging red, green, and blue light produces the visible spectrum.

CMYK is a subtractive model used in printing. Cyan, magenta, and yellow are used to produce colors of the visible spectrum.

Red, Yellow, Blue (RYB) system is a subtractive model used for pigment mixing. It is commonly known as the standard color wheel of the visible spectrum. Red, yellow, and blue form the primary colors; violet (or purple), orange, and green form the secondary colors. This subtractive system implies that the mixture of two colors cannot produce a third color that is greater in saturation than the two parent colors. For example, mixing yellow and blue to achieve green will result in a third color that is perceived as a dull, desaturated green rather than the expected colorful green hue.

The hues that define a color wheel derived from pigment progress in an orderly sequence related to the visible spectrum. These colors also progress in a value sequence of light to dark.

RYB color system is a subtractive model. Red, yellow, and blue are the primary colors of the commonly known color wheel. The secondary colors—violet, orange, and green—make up a secondary triad. In theory, the secondary colors are produced by mixing equal amounts of red and blue, red and yellow, and blue and yellow. Since this is a subtractive process, this method of mixing produces desaturated secondary colors.

This color wheel illustrates an arrangement of primary, secondary, and tertiary colors of the red, yellow, and blue color system.

This color wheel illustrates an arrangement of primary, secondary, and tertiary colors of the red, green, and blue color system.

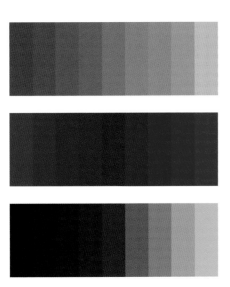

Colors that reside opposite one another on the color wheel are called complementary. In this illustration, the primary and secondary colors form a complementary pair. Colors that are absolutely balanced in temperature contrast will yield a chromatic gray color when the pairs are neutralized. If the colors are not absolutely balanced in temperature contrast, the third neutral color appears brown. The derivative colors between the two full chroma hues are desaturated tonal colors.

Theoretically, the neutral gray should be the same color since the complementary pairs are derived from one primary and one secondary color. That is true if the secondary colors were actually derived from two primaries. Because pigment mixing is a subtractive process, the secondary colors would be desaturated. The grays are different due to the formation of pigments based on chemistry that produces fully saturated colors.

Another method of manipulating the saturation level of a fully saturated hue is to modify it with a neutral gray. These examples show a fully saturated color mixed with a neutral gray. Since yellow is lighter in value and blue is darker in value than the neutral gray, the units of contrast are strong. Since the orange is similar in value to the neutral gray, the units contrast in saturation but remain constant in value.

 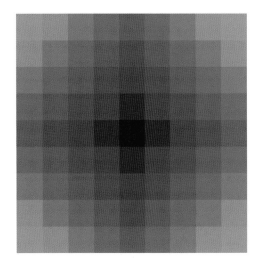

While color systems purposefully specify colors in an orderly sequential visual arrangement, their appearance is dependent upon specific environments. All colors transform in appearance when the context or environment changes. A color placed upon a light background will appear dark. When the same color is placed upon a dark background it will appear light. Similarly, a color placed upon a background low in saturation will appear greater in saturation than when it's placed upon a highly saturated color background. The perceptual effect is called **simultaneous contrast**. Since colors are rarely seen in isolation, the effect of simultaneous contrast causes the appearance of colors to change in a given palette or harmony.

There are twelve units in this white-to-black value scale. The center strip is one value of gray but appears to change in value from dark to light. Comparatively, light colors make a color appear dark and dark colors make that same color appear light.

Value changes affect the appearance of size, shape, and space. Each rectangular unit in the twelve-step scale appears concave. The strip through the center of the value scale appears convex. This visual effect is due to our conventional expectation of a light source originating from above, as does the Sun. A light source above an object will create a shadow underneath. In the twelve-step value scale, the dark edge of each unit is at the top and the light edge at the bottom. Light from above reflects from the bottom edge of the rectangle while the top edge is dark shadow. As the brain assumes a single light source, value gradation produces a three-dimensional shape.

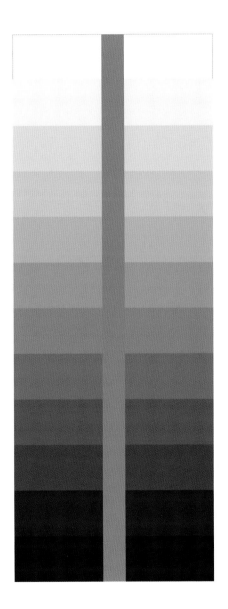

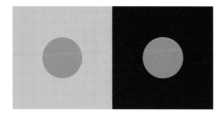

The two circle figures are the same color. Perceptually, they appear to change in hue family as one appears green and the other yellow-green. This is due to the figure color resting on one field of orange that is similar to its hue family, and the blue field contrasting the figure's hue family.

The two circle figures are the same color. Perceptually, they appear to change in saturation, as one appears more colorful than the other. This is the result of a color figure positioned on a desaturated field of color and the same figure color positioned on a saturated field of color.

Simultaneous contrast also affects the appearance of color brightness in different contexts. White's illusion illustrates the fact that the same luminance can elicit different perceptions of brightness.

White's illusion is sometimes combined with the Munker illusion that uses colors instead of gray scale.

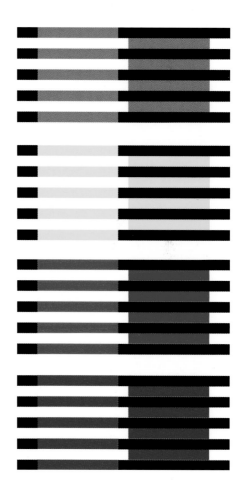

Another perceptual phenomenon related to simultaneous contrast is the negative afterimage effect. When viewing a hue for twenty to thirty seconds, the rods and cones become fatigued. Once this occurs, the inverse, or complement color will appear when the eyes are shifted to a white surface. Every color has a complementary color opposite. While the perception of different individuals may vary, the after-effect images seen is consistent.

Employing gridlike structures of color, line, and shape is a common practice when organizing space. However, these structures have visual consequences. These organizational structures generate disturbing optical effects caused by physiological reactions to visual stimuli in the brain. These effects present serious challenges for designers to consider when organizing elements within the image area. The Hermann and Scintillating grids are two examples that illustrate this point.

In the **Hermann Grid**, the black-and-white squares on a white background create the appearance of fluctuating white or gray shapes at the intersections of the white lines.

In the **Scintillating Grid**, dots seem to appear and disappear at the intersections of two lines crossing each other vertically and diagonally. When focusing on a single intersection, the dot disappears.

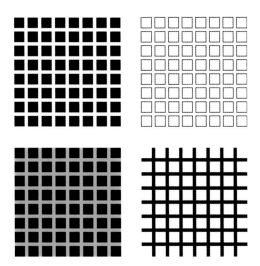

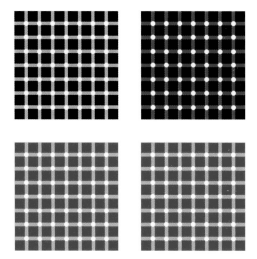

The Hermann Grid produces negative afterimages of disappearing dots in the intersections of lines in the field of white, gray, or black.

The Scintillating Grid produces negative afterimages of disappearing dots in the intersections of vertical and diagonal lines in the white, gray, black, or color fields.

There are five units of color used in this optical color mixture study. The five colors are shown in the bottom horizontal strip. In each of the four horizontal bands of color, the same five colors are used throughout. Comparing the horizontal bands, note the changes in hue, value, and saturation of the five colors. Since the blue and green pair is similar in value and saturation contrast, they appear to blend as one color field.

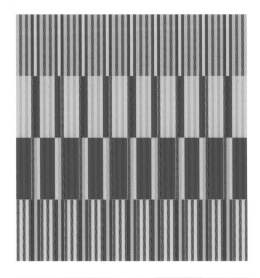

Design: Kathryn Lee

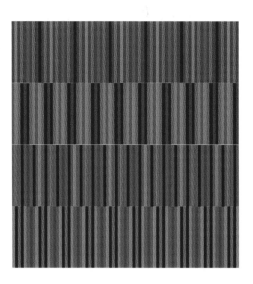

Design: Laura Frycek

Color systems provide the substance for developing a color harmony. But they do not provide a method of making color choices. Forming a color harmony or palette is a matter of exercising restraint by controlling the hue, value, and saturation.

The control of hue is dependent upon the number used. More than five hue families tend to create visual clutter. Controlling value and saturation are contingent upon decisive contrast. However, ordering these color variables is incidental to image context and message. Applying color according to its visual importance or dominance is essential for clear communication. This is accomplished by objective analytical reasoning—comparing the similarity and contrasting relationships of hue, value, and saturation.

Colors that are equal in value may contrast in saturation. A fully saturated yellow is light in value. A fully saturated violet is perceived as a dark value.

When comparing two colors for similarity in value, they must be placed adjacent to each other. Squint at the edge where the two colors meet for approximately twenty seconds. If the edge blurs, the colors are similar in value. If they are not the same in value, the two colors will become noticeably dark and light.

Also important to communicating a message is evoking an emotional response. This process of color selection correlates to subjective analytical reasoning—the feeling that a color combination elicits.

Design: Matt Puhalla

A composition of color shapes is organized to enhance the color in the leaf. The composition above modifies the value of the colors to be equal. Contrast is maintained in saturation and hue. In the third composition, the saturation of the colors is modified to remain similar. Contrast is maintained in hue and value. The final study illustrates similarity in hue. In this study, contrast is maintained through value and saturation contrast of a green hue, creating a monochromatic color harmony.

Munsell Color Notation System

To assist in the assessment of value and saturation contrast, it is helpful to refer to a color system with a pragmatic and useful organizational structure. The Munsell Color Notation System employs a color space based on the three dimensions of color—hue, value, and chroma. While Albert Munsell designed this system through extensive user testing around 1910, it is still used today in design, anthropology, and science. Specifically, the NASA Ames Research Center applies Munsell principles to understand perceptual color relationships and to assist in the design of color combinations that are legible.

Munsell organized color on a vertical center axis. Each unit of color in the vertical column is perceptually uniform in light to dark contrast within the same hue family.

The chroma axis extends from the central axis at a right angle. The full chroma hue is positioned according to a value equal to the central axis gray scale. From the central neutral gray scale, the colors are organized in a number of gradients of equal degrees of saturation contrast. The horizontal rows form units of color uniform in chroma/saturation with no contrast in their value.

Every hue family in the Munsell ordering system characterizes an objective color harmony. Color harmonies comprise two fundamentally inseparable ingredients—similarity and contrast.

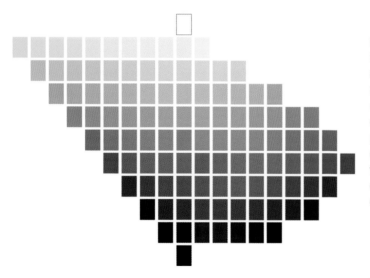

From the Munsell Color Notation System, two hues—yellow and blue—are illustrated. The full chroma yellow is defined as equal to gray at the ninth unit value and is positioned at the full chroma unit. The full chroma blue is defined as equal to the fourth unit value, neutral gray, and is positioned at the full saturation unit. Within each of the two hue families, colors are organized as vertical columns that are structured in value contrast, top to bottom. Saturation contrast is confined within the same rows, left to right.

Value or saturation scales generated by software programs will not produce the appearance of an evenly graduated scale. Gradations and blends in software programs are based on precise mathematical models. However, visually they do not appear accurate.

Intrinsic Color Structure

Interpreting and understanding a visual message involves deliberate control of mass/space elements and their attributes. Simply being sensitive to the visual complexities and conditions of color is fundamental to generating a clear visual message.

Color requires thoughtful application, therefore, it is imperative to place it in a structured context. Color serves as an activating stimulus that intensifies visual consciousness and responsiveness—it conjures emotions and reinforces visual information processing and meaning. When color is thoughtfully organized and applied, it has been demonstrated that it substantially improves communication and comprehension. The three properties of color have the potential to form an ordered visual language that establish meaning and evoke emotion.

As an intrinsic visual attribute of form, color functions as language and message. Controlling the visual relationships of hue, value, and saturation contrast can significantly assist a person's cognitive ability to assign importance to an object.

There are some who hypothesize the mind's eye does not readily give a visual ordering to colors, but ineffective use of color always generates confusion and ambiguity. By executing control of hue, value, and saturation, the mind's eye does readily perceive visual order.

Perceiving and understanding the order and importance of color interaction has useful applications. Color adds significance to visual communication as it accentuates and makes perceptible the identification of that which is perceived first, as the main idea, before decoding additional elements in the message. Perceived hierarchy represents a sequence of visual commands in the language of color. It's significant in signaling systems, wayfinding systems, maps, instrumentation, educational, instructional material, and so on. Effective color communication permits users to view, retrieve, access, decipher, interpret, understand, and experience a variety of information systems in a meaningful, valid, and authentic manner.

Applying rational principles of color organization offers credible objective criteria for choosing a color palette. Color structures contain patterns of intrinsic visual harmony. Color harmonies have an internal orderly structure composed of a dynamic balance between similar and contrasting parts. The end result is a congruent and pleasing arrangement of parts.

The intrinsic structure of the color's properties provides the foundation of a visual language. The visual language of color is formed by inherent oservable characteristics of color systems. Interestingly, these inherent color combinations are found in nature as well. Innumerable color configurations can be formulated by eight conventional color harmonies. Thoughtful manipulation of the properties within a conventional color harmony presents a powerful means of communication. Each property of color intrinsically governs the rules of order.

The conventional color harmonies include:

MONOCHROMATIC	PRIMARY	SECONDARY	TERTIARY	COMPLEMENTARY	SPLIT COMPLEMENTS	ANALOGOUS	DIVERGENT
1	2	3	4	5	6	7	8

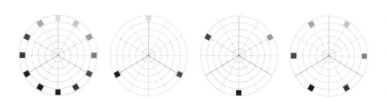

The colors represented in this system make up a twelve-step arrangement of the visible spectrum. This make-up includes the primary, secondary, and tertiary color groups.

The monochromatic harmonies are broken into two categories of value and saturation. In a monochromatic harmony, colors remain within the same hue family. The derivative colors in the hue family appear to be mixtures of white or black. This structure establishes contrast in value and no contrast in hue.

The saturation category does something similar. But, rather than using white or black as modifiers, a gray value is used instead. As with the value structure, there is a contrast in saturation and no contrast in hue.

All hues in the visible spectrum may be constituted as a monochromatic color harmony by employing this method.

This color structure illustrates tints of the primary and secondary colors. White is the additive color, producing derivatives from the full color to white located at the center point.

Derivative tints and shades of the orange hue represent a monochromatic harmony.

This color structure illustrates shades of the primary and secondary colors. Black is the additive color, producing derivatives from the full color to black located at the center point.

Derivative tones of the orange hue form a monochromatic harmony.

This color structure illustrates tones of the primary and secondary colors. Gray is the additive color, producing derivatives from the full color to gray located at the center point.

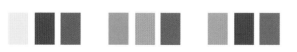

Derivative tones and values of the orange hue form a monochromatic harmony.

Primary Harmony: red—yellow—blue

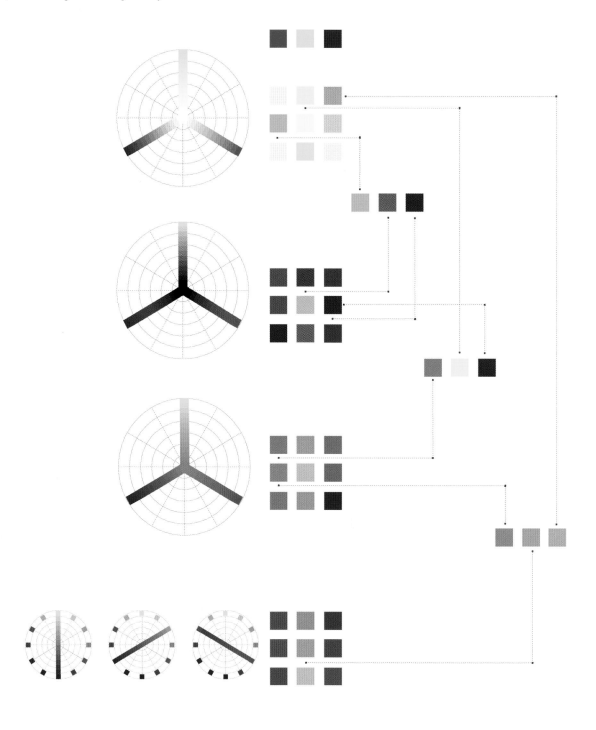

The primary harmony and its derivative color structure utilize tints, shades, and tones. Note that tones may also be generated from the mixture of complementary colors. Complements are colors directly across from each other on the color wheel. If the complementary pair is precisely opposite each other, the derivative colors will ultimately move to a chromatic gray color. If the colors are not precisely opposite, the derivatives will ultimately yield brown. By arranging a complementary pair from each tint, shade, and tonal category, a multitude of color combinations can be achieved within the primary color harmony.

Secondary Harmony: orange–violet–green

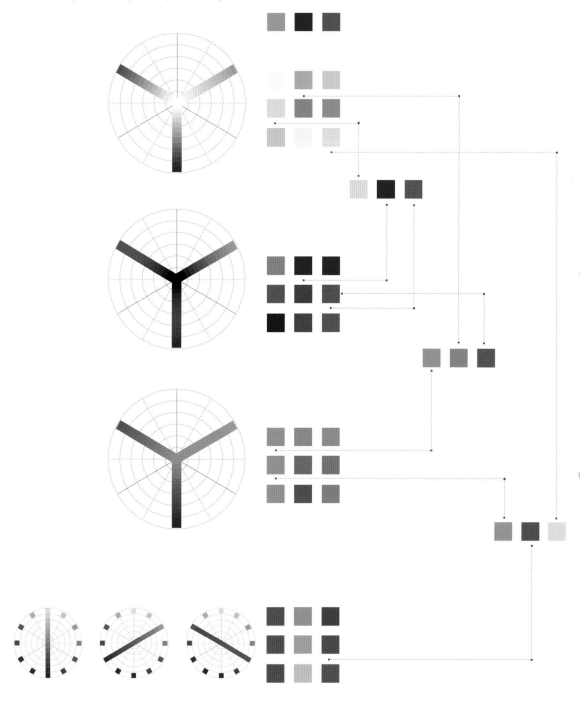

The secondary harmony is defined by its derivative color structure applying tints, shades, and tones. As with the primary harmonies, a multitude of color combinations can be achieved within the secondary color harmony.

Tertiary Harmony: equally spaced between primary colors

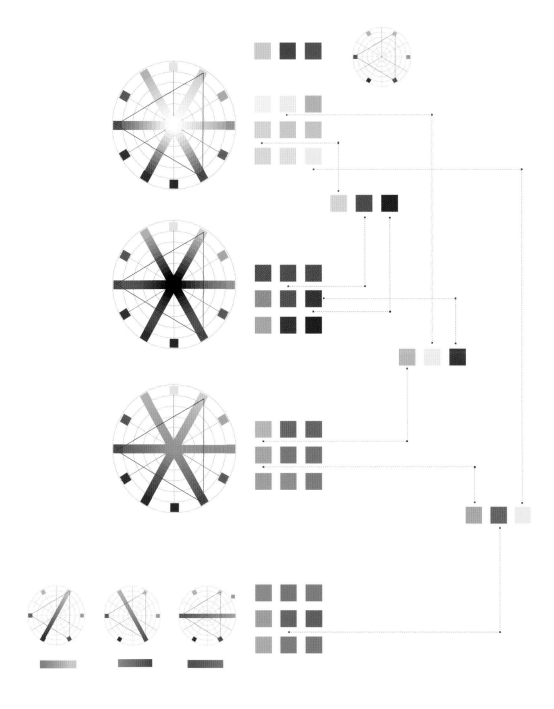

One set of tertiary colors—yellow-orange—red-violet—blue-green is
used. The derivative color structure applies tints, shades, and tones.
By locating derivative colors from the tint, shade, and tonal categories,
the number of combinations is endless within the tertiary color harmony.

Tertiary Harmony: equally spaced between secondary colors

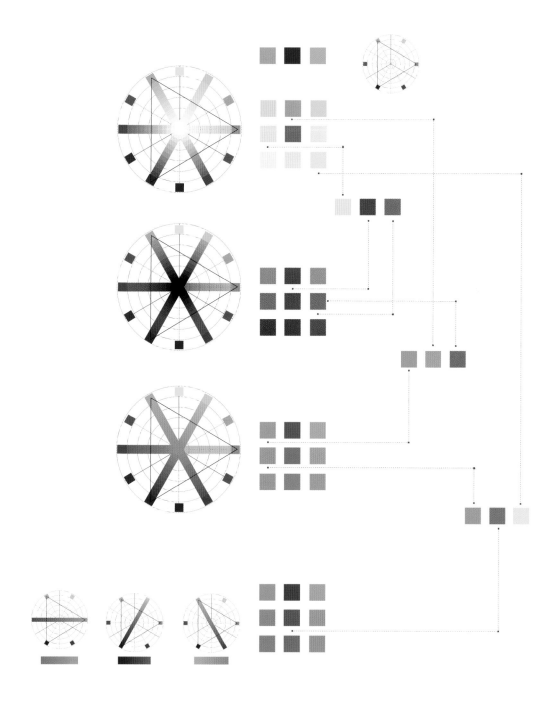

One set of tertiary colors—red-orange–blue-violet–yellow-green is used. The derivative color structure applies tints, shades, and tones.

Intrinsic Color Structure

Analogous Harmony: adjacent colors in a limited range on the color wheel

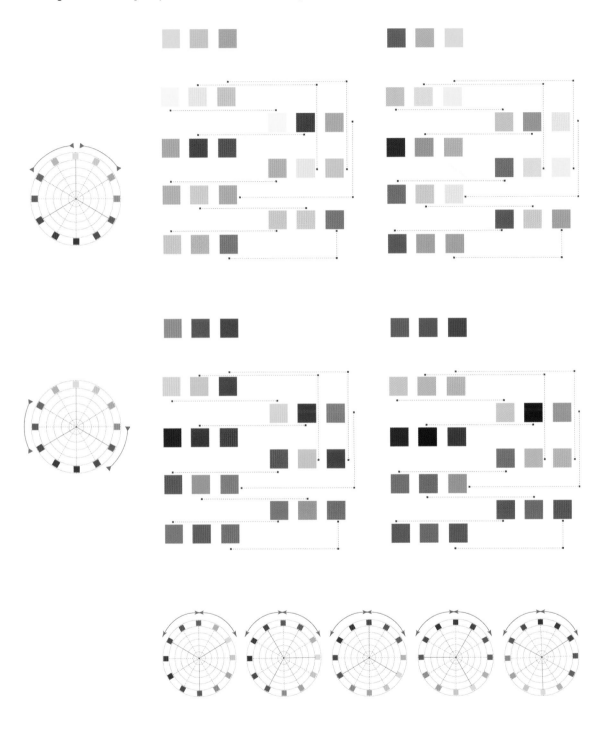

This example shows a set of four different analogous
harmonies and their derivative colors. Derivatives
are the result of tints, shades, and tonal mixtures.

The colors in the four corners of these studies contrast in relative or absolute temperature. In the first example the yellow-green is cool compared to the red in the upper-right corner. The yellow-green becomes warm when comparing it to the bottom-left corner that is blue.

Within each of the three studies, colors share a similarity in value and saturation. The contrasting property is hue. When value and saturation are equal, no one color is more important than the other.

Design: Darrin Hunter, Mark Grote, Laura Frycek

Arcos de Valdevez, Portugal
One predominate color provides a context for the letter slot, door handle, lock, and window panes.

Obidos, Portugal
Minimal usage of the blue stripe is a focal point in an environment of various warm and cool neutral tones.

Lisbon, Portugal
The blue decorative geometry is a focal point in a building's façade composed of gray neutral tones.

Photographs: Diane Lee

Photograph: Diane Lee

Lisbon, Portugal
The primary color harmony defines the compositional structure of the image. The proportional relationships of shape and color are clearly articulated. The desaturated, light value red, a desaturated, dark value yellow, and a saturated blue triangle frame the wind-blown clothing.

The primary and secondary colors are naturally associated with the color wheel when they are represented at full chroma. This magazine cover and poster from the Hirshhorn Museum communicate a message clearly in sync with the museum's purpose. Note also the division of the image area is structured in proportional rectangular shapes.

Design:
Chermayeff & Geismar, New York

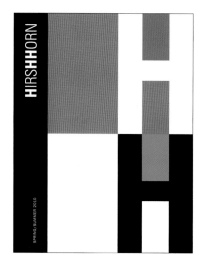

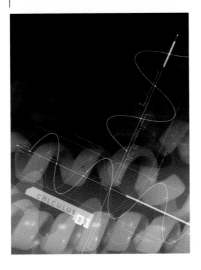 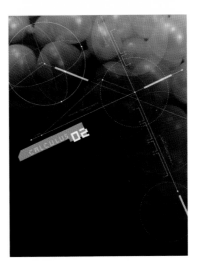 

The three book cover studies illustrate a monochromatic color harmony. Note the surface area quantity of the hue appears to occupy less than half of the image area. The monochromatic area serves as a background for the typography and graphic content, which resides at the top of the visual hierarchy.

Design: Katrina Mendoza

Cooper-Hewitt, National Design Museum employs color as a visual means to define content in the *Why Design Now?* 2010 National Design Triennial catalogue. A color palette classifies categories in the catalogue. Because the colors share a common degree of saturation and similarity in value, no one area is more important than any other. The primary and secondary color palette establishes a context appropriate to the content. The alternating sequence of warm and cool colors provides enough visual contrast to distinguish each category.

Design: Steff Geissbuhler
C&G Partners, New York

The logo design for the Darien Library is composed of a monochromatic color harmony. Arranging the value and saturation structure in a consistent sequence suggests the movement of pages in a book. This structured approach to color and shape presents an image of action and a positive message. Note the implied circle arcs that suggest flat shapes forming a spatial plane representing pages of the book.

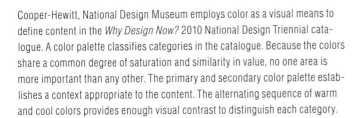

Design: Michael Bierut and Yve Ludwig
Pentagram Design, New York

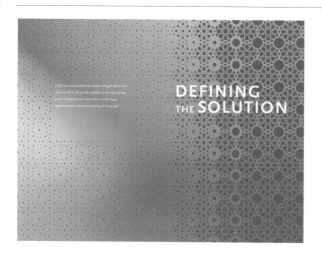

Cultural motifs are interpreted through color, point, line, and shape in these spreads for a book. Derivatives of the primary colors are used. The gold-toned gradients are derivatives of a yellow hue.

The content and contexts communicate the vibrancy of the women and culture portrayed as well as contributing to the hopeful tone of the book. The traditional patterns are used in dynamic ways to convey the idea of change. Shapes defined by their interior linear pattern create a symbol for cycles—one is fading while the other is strong. The pattern itself stresses interconnectivity.

Design: Allison Leidy

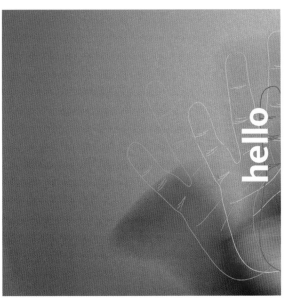
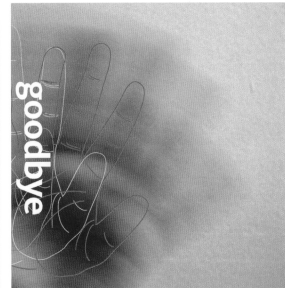

The primary color harmony employed in this book spread uses derivatives of red. These derivative colors produce a gradients suggesting movement. The red, yellow, blue harmony is lively and welcoming in its contextual feel.

Design: Lindsey N. Meyer

4

"There is no work of art without system."

—Le Corbusier

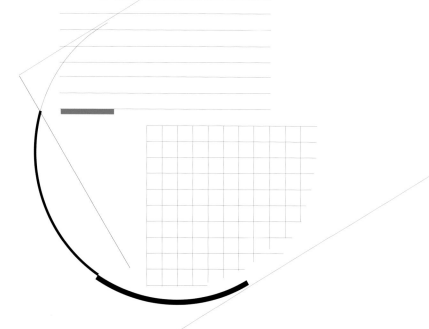

Spatial Structure

image area and the implied forces

ORDER

Spatial Structure | ORDER

Proportion

Without proportion, form is meaningless. Our visual intelligence is dependent upon it. Proportion accords order, structure, harmony, and gives shape to the image area. Implicitly and explicitly, proportion defines the division of space within the image area and establishes visual balance. Proportions are mathematic and harmonic.

Proportional relationships are inherently integrated into the context of all objects including nature. In the built environment, proportional divisions of space may be easily identified and visually apparent. In nature, the proportional divisions are hidden and implied. The division of space is the result of decision-making processes conditioned by our visual experiences and interaction with objects. Raising the level of awareness about hidden and implied proportion is a useful contributing determinate in ordering and structuring space. Imposed limitations of spatial divisions create limitless organizational possibilities.

Proportion is a comparison of one surface area to another. Proportions are expressed in ratios. Dividing a square into two equal parts creates a proportional relationship among three parts—two rectangles and the square itself. The two rectangles are proportionally the same. A single rectangle is in a 1:2 ratio with the square. Comparisons of dissimilar shapes can be made in terms of proportional relationships. The circle's rectangle and triangle is a good example.

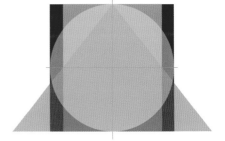

The circle's rectangle and triangle dates to classical Greek geometry. It is a proportional relationship of parts that are the same in surface area. The circle, rectangle, and square are harmoniously balanced and proportionate. Placing the circle inside the all-important square is the starting point for this illustration. Eliminating one tenth of the square creates a rectangle in proportion to the circle. Extending lines from the center point of the rectangle's top, left, and right sides creates a triangle in proportion to the circle and rectangle.

Symmetry

Once an image area has been defined as the compositional whole, the first element placed within that area divides the space proportionally. This, and the subsequent divisions that follow, are critical. Order and unity within the space depends on the balance of all parts that make the whole. Balance is directly related to the Gestalt Law of Symmetry—symmetrical images are perceived collectively. By its very nature, symmetry implies balance of parts that form the whole.

Order in symmetry may be visually obvious or hidden. Bilateral and radial symmetry are the most common types in which the order of parts is predictably regular. It is readily apparent in design, art, and architecture. Symmetrical changes are figure transformations that include repetition and movement. Typically, size remains constant, while position, number, and orientation change. Symmetry operations defining repetition and movement include glide-reflection, glide-rotation, reflection, rotation, and translation. Glide reflections involve more than one operation. Balance among the parts is visually stable since the parts are proportionally repetitive.

Translation symmetry is a movement without rotating or reflecting—it implies direction and distance.

Reflection is bilateral symmetry, which is a mirror image.

Rotation symmetry revolves around a central point.

Glide reflection involves more than one symmetry operation.

The inherent forces of the square are the foundation of most proportional systems. While letterforms in themselves tend to be asymmetrical, the **bilateral symmetry** of the square is critical to letterform design. Letterforms designed using geometry can be traced to the Italian Renaissance. In a manuscript defining the rules governing the construction of the Roman alphabet, Felice Feliciano established mathematical proportions for letterforms. Consistent, harmonious typographic families share the same heights, weights, and general proportions.

While bilateral symmetry balances the space with equal-size units, **dynamic symmetry** creates the appearance of asymmetrical parts. Dynamic symmetry is a system of shapes that appears to be asymmetrical. It is a proportional division of form and space often hidden beneath the object's surface. Its visual harmony consists of different parts formed by mathematical relationships working in unison.

This type of symmetrical order is found in the natural environment. These organic symmetries influence our cognitive reasoning, which in turn affects our aesthetic preferences and processes. Being willfully aware of the hidden structural order found in our natural surroundings provides invaluable insight into our intuitive subjective inclinations and tendencies.

Ancient Greek mathematicians observed a golden ratio appearing frequently in the proportions found in geometry. The **golden ratio** or **golden section**, as it is known, may be described by comparing parts. Literally, the golden section is stated as— the lesser part is to the greater part as the greater part is to the whole. Each unit is directly proportional to the others. Internally, a rectangle in the golden section proportion produces an internal and external spiral. In geometry, a golden spiral is a logarithmic spiral. Its successive growth factor is related to the golden ratio. Relatively, a golden spiral gets proportionally wider for every quarter turn it makes.

It is generally believed that this proportion system is aesthetically pleasing to the eye. The golden section proportion was employed in the architecture, sculpture, and artifacts of the classical Greek period.

Luca Pacioli designed letters derived from the square and circle.

Many fifth-century Greek vessels are in the proportion of the golden section.

A lowercase *a* from Adobe Caslon Pro, superimposed onto the square and circle

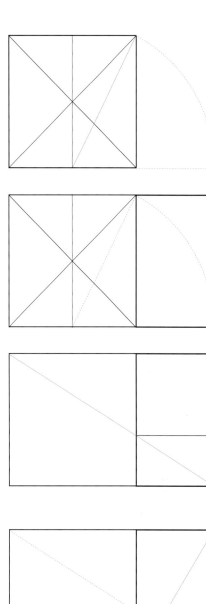

The rectangle in the proportion of the golden section begins with a square. The distance between the center of the base of the square to the corner creates a line length that is used to establish the rectangle. By extending this new line from the center of the base of the square the length of a new rectangle is defined in proportion to the golden section: The new small rectangle is to the square as the square is to the large rectangle.

The diagonal of the large rectangle divides the line between the square and small rectangle, forming a smaller square and rectangle. The new parts are in harmony with the whole. The lesser parts are to the greater parts as the greater parts are to the whole.

The diagonal of the small rectangle is used to define another division. Alternating between the two rectangles and dividing the smallest unit create the new divisions. All units are in harmony with the golden section. Note that the two intersecting diagonals form a right angle.

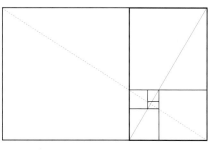

A quarter arc generates a decreasing spiral. Each segment of the circle diminishes in its size proportionally as it moves toward the smallest unit.

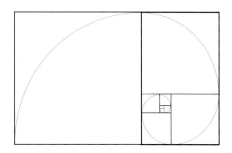

115

Divine Proportion

Numerous artists and architects have proportioned
their works to approximate the golden ratio. Directly
associated with the golden section is a numerical
system known as the divine proportion. Mathematically, the proportion is known as *phi*, which equals
1.618. This number is derived from the Fibonocci
numerical sequence.

The **Fibonacci sequence** is the numerical series
1, 1, 2, 3, 5, 8, 13, 21, 34, 55, 89, 144, and is generated
by the rule: [$f1 = f2 = 1$, $fn+1 = fn+fn-1$]. Fibonacci
of Pisa introduced the series in a problem involv-
ing the growth of a population of rabbits. Each
number in the sequence is the sum of the two
preceding numbers.

Examples of the divine proportion can be found in
architecture, art, music, and symbols. The dimensions of the pyramids of Egypt, the Greek Parthenon,
and a few classical revival and contemporary build-
ings employ the divine proportion.

The divine proportion is also considered to be a
fundamental building block in nature. Subsequently,
the world and nature have an underlying proportional
order. Humans, animals, plants, and aspects of the
universe all share a common dimensional proportion
that is found in the phi ratio: 1 to 1.68.

The ratio of each spiral's diameter in a nautilus
shell is equal to phi—1 to 1.68. Sunflower seeds grow
spirals in which the rotation of each diameter to the
next is 1 to 1.68. Spiraled pinecone petals and leaf
positioning on plant stalks follow the ratio of the
divine proportion.

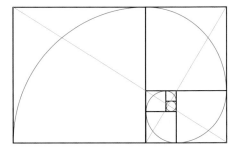

The Fiboncci proportion is a numerical series
generating numbers 1, 1, 2, 3, 5, 8, 13. The succession of numbers is achieved by adding the
last two numbers in the sequence.

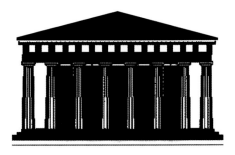

The Parthenon is an example of classical Greek
architecture in the divine proportion.

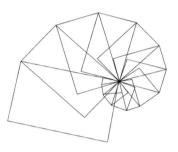

These illustrations are examples of the divine proportion found frequently in nature. In the sunflower example, the arrangement of seeds is known to be the most efficient way of filling the space. In addition to the nautilus shell spiral being in the 1:1.6 proportion, note that the rectangles that rotate around a point are also in the same proportion.

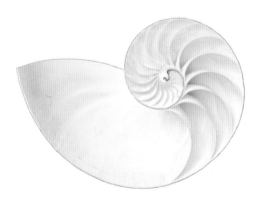

The interior and exterior of the nautilus shell are directly related to the spiral and proportion of the 1:1.6 ratio.

While there is no definitive proof, the golden ratio also appears in music. Musical works by composers Mozart, Beethoven, Bartók, Debussy, and Schubert may have utilized the proportion. This was accomplished through sectional divisions in a musical composition and possibly through harmonic structuring.

Da Vinci's Vitruvian Man provides the perfect example of his interest in proportion. Da Vinci demonstrated through Vitruvian Man the structure of the human body in proportional ratios equal to phi as follows:

* the distance from the tip of the head to the floor divided by the distance from the navel to the floor

* from the shoulder to fingertips divided by the distance from the elbow to fingertips

* from the hip to the floor divided by the knee to the floor

* divisions of finger joints, toes, and spinal cord

The field of anthropometry was created in order to describe individual human proportion variations.

In addition, the proportion is the root of the pentagon and five-pointed star. The five-pointed star is one of the most powerful images found in ancient history as it was considered to be both divine and magical by many cultures.

The late twentieth-century architect and artist, Le Corbusier, developed a proportional system called Le Modulor. In Le Corbusier's model, the height of the human body is divided by the golden section at the navel. The proportional model employs the square and golden section as a theoretical modular system.

The Le Modulor system was developed to relate human proportions in the design of products and architecture. The intent of the proportional model is to provide a system of logic, function, and visual aesthetics.

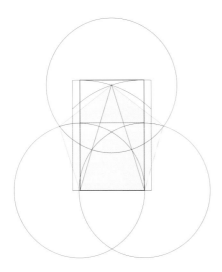

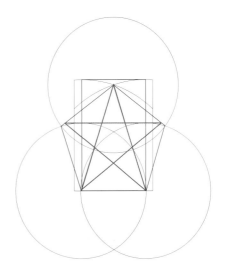

The first drawing demonstrates the way a pentagon can be formed by applying the divine proportion. In the second drawing, the pentagon generates the five-pointed star.

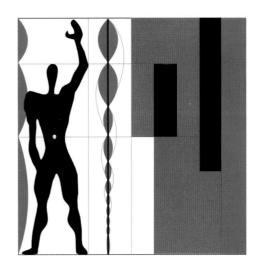

Da Vinci's Vitruvian Man is an example of the 1:1.6 ratio applied to the proportions of the human figure. Da Vinci illustrated various parts of the human body in the same proportion.

The architect Le Corbusier developed his proportional system called Le Modulor in the tradition of DaVinci's Vitruvian Man. Le Modulor is an anthropometric scale of human proportions for the purpose of improving the appearance and function of architecture.

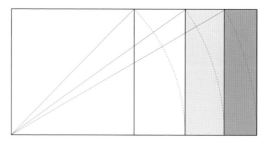

Root rectangles are another means of defining a rectangle of proportional relevance. Root rectangles begin with a square, which produces a sequence of rectangles that successively increases in one direction in an arithmetic sequence of rectangular parts. An arithmetic sequence is a succession of numbers that moves from one term to the next by adding the same value. For example, a numerical sequence of [1, 2, 3] or [2, 4, 6] would be an arithmetic sequence since the value between the subsequent numbers is constant.

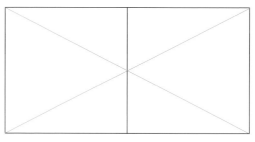

The inherent diagonal of the square is used to produce the length of the first rectangle. Successively, the diagonals of each new rectangle generate the next rectangle in a square root arithmetic sequence.

Successively employing the diagonal of each rectangle will produce a new rectangle. Each rectangle increases in size in an arithmetic progression in a square root proportion √2, √3, √4. At the √4 proportion, the original square is doubled.

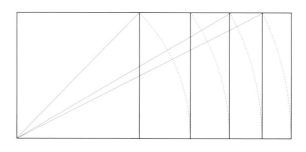

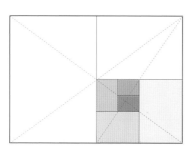

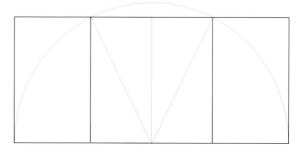

The dynamic rectangle in the root 2 proportion is constructed by using the diagonal of the square. Subdividing the rectangle into smaller proportional rectangular units is derived from two diagonals. As the rectangles get smaller, they remain the same root 2 proportion.

The root 5 proportion produces a golden section proportion that is bilaterally symmetrical. The square is centered with two rectangles in the 1:1.6 ratio on either side.

The proportions of the root 2 rectangle form the basis of a system used in standard ISO paper sizes A, B, and C. This ratio is a convenient paper size since dividing the format into two equal pieces will result in a format with the same width/height ratio.

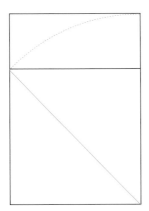

Proportion is critical for creating a visually pleasing and functional page layout. Since the time of Gutenberg, it's not unusual to find books printed in a vertical position that conforms precisely or loosely to the golden section. Root rectangles and golden section proportions have been used to standardize paper sizes.

The principles of proportion for page design were defined in the mid-to-late twentieth century. Variations on these principles have evolved over the decades.

Early in the twentieth century, paper proportions were systemized into a model that would accommodate different paper sizes. The system was introduced as a DIN standard. The standard proportions are based on the square. The side of square in relation to its diagonal determines a rectangular format. This is the same proportion as the root rectangle—root 2. The advantage of this system is scaling. Each time a format in this proportion is divided into equal halves, the subsequent sizes remain proportionally equal.

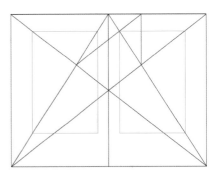

Known as the *Van de Graaf Canon*, Van de Graaf devised this construction of a two-page layout based upon the diagonals of the rectangles. No matter the size of the page, the Van de Graaf Canon always results in the top left corner of the text block being one ninth from the top and one ninth from the inside margin. This system ensured that the text block will be positioned with consistency, balance, and harmony.

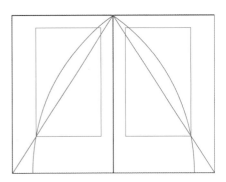

Recognizing the importance of the long forgotten *Van de Graaf Canon*, Jan Tschiclod resurrected the proportional system in the early to mid-twentieth century. In his publication, *The Design of the Book*, Swiss typographer and modernist designer, Jan Tschichold, proportioned page layout in approximation to the golden section.

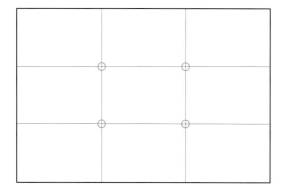

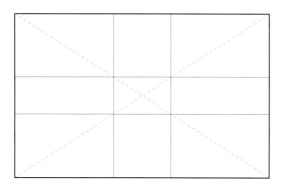

A simplified version of the golden section is the "rule of thirds." Oddly, it is not a rule at all. Rather, it is a "rule of thumb" associated with capturing photographic images. Since the golden section is believed to be the ideal proportional aesthetic, the proportional divisions of a rectangular format are divided into a grid of nine equal units approximately in similar proportions to the golden section.

The grid is initially intended to assist the compositional arrangement of parts in a camera's view finder. The nine parts of the divided rectangle allow for positioning and isolating the focal point of a scene at intersections of equally spaced horizontal and vertical lines. The proportional divisions allow for framing an image in golden mean–like proportions.

The grid of nine rectangles presents an opportunity for creating a static or dynamic image. Framing a composition for effective communication depends on many factors including the elements, the attributes, and our perceptual structures. Context and content are the preeminent concerns when deciding upon compositional arrangement of parts.

These drawings illustrate the similarities between the image area of photographic proportions and the golden section rectangle. In the first drawing, the dimensions of 35-mm film are formatted in its 3:2 ratio. In the second drawing, the golden section is divided using the rule of thirds in its 1:1.6 ratio.

Since proportion is a comparison of surface areas, a grid system of fixed horizontal and vertical divisions can be useful in determining relationships between the parts of the image area format. A grid-based system enhances organization. It provides a visual and structural balance that brings continuity to the image area. Grids have been in use since the thirteenth century when scribes used the Villard grid to organize their handwritten manuscripts.

The grid is a plan that helps provide continuity among the elements. It is an organizational structure that helps to unify the elements within the image area. The grid can be rigid and static or rhythmic and dynamic. The beauty of a grid lies in its flexibility. When used properly, it will enrich the visual experience and make it easy for the viewer to understand content. Imposing a grid system should never impede creativity.

Grid structures can be fluid and provide opportunities for contrast in size, sequence, interval, number, density, orientation, and position. In order to avoid chaos and create compositional harmony, grid structures provide opportunities for continuity, similarity, grouping, alignment, transitions, connections, and terminations.

As noted with other elements and attributes of form, grid proportions should be based on content and context. The context of some situations calls for concise and deliberate communication, while other contextual situations call for layers of hierarchical information organization.

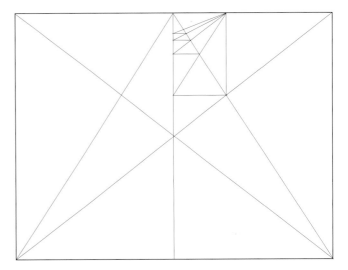

Villard devised the system dividing a straight line into logical and harmonious parts consisting of thirds, fourths, fifths, to infinity.

The Fibonacci proportion defines the rectangle in this illustration. The grid is derived from the base square of the Fibonacci proportion. The divisions of space remain consistent with the proportional units of the system.

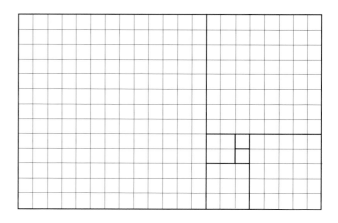

The divisions of space within the rectangle can be static if there is no contrast in the mass/ space elements, their attributes, and perceived structure. In this example, there is contrast in size, shape, weight, and direction. The use of figure/ground reversal, repetition, position, proximity, trajectories, and closure are also a factor contributing to visual interest.

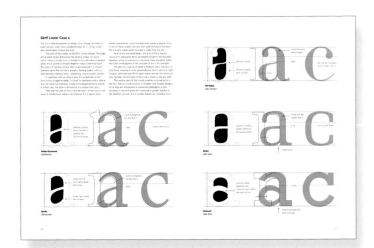

In the book, *Designing Type*, author Karen Cheng demonstrates the visual principles of letter construction. Optical effects of shape and form consistency, proportional systems for type structure, and legibility within a type-face are fundamental issues of typography.

Design: Karen Cheng

Cheng's poster defining letter construction divides the image area into proportionally equal horizontal bands. Both the vertical and horizontal divisions of space are an appropriate context for understanding letterform design.

Design: Laura Frycek

Design: Lisa Bambach

In the typographic grid studies that follow, typography is used as line and shape, which defines the proportion of the page. Bold type provides contrast to the blocks of type that read as gray textured values.

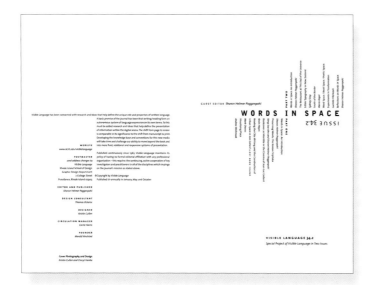

Design: Kristin Cullen

Words inhabit space in horizontal and vertical directions in this *Visible Language* layout by Kristin Cullen. The layout explores a balance between the practical and the poetic. Each page is divided in the same proportion, with a square at the bottom and a rectangle at the top. A line of type defines the top edge of a square in the left layout and a bold font is employed to define the top of the square in the layout on the right.

Design: Kristin Cullen

Because the poster contains a great deal of content that must communicate meaningful information, it is necessary to structure consistent proportional columns and a baseline grid. To provide visual interest, contrast of shape, texture, color, and typographic elements are strategically placed within the system. The angles employed in the composition are inherently connected to the proportions of the horizontal and vertical divisions of the space.

Photograph: D. M. Puhalla

The use of a proportional system along with a grid does not in itself guarantee a visually successful composition. Proportions and grids form the foundation of an ordered structural system that has the potential to unify the parts of the whole. Structural systems are based upon context and content supporting a logical objective rationale for design organization. And, design organization is the product of thoughtful and purposeful arrangement of the mass/space elements, their attributes, and their perceived structures.

The rule of thirds is applied in the vertical orientation of the composition. This division of space follows the principles of proportion established in the golden mean.

Photograph: D. M. Puhalla

"The grid system is an aid, not a guarantee. It permits a number of possible uses and each designer can look for a solution appropriate to his personal style. But one must learn how to use the grid; it is an art that requires practice."

—Josef Müller-Brockmann

In this photographic composition, the points of interest are the three boats that form an implied triangle. The points of interest in the composition are roughly horizontal lines or shapes that interact with the three rectangular divisions of the image area formed by the rule of thirds.

5

"The essence is to give order to information, form to ideas, expression and feeling to artifacts that document human experience."

—Phillip Meggs

Ordering Strategy

Ordering Strategy

Forming a systematic approach to the organization of space requires thoughtful and focused planning. The mass/space elements and their variables comprise all the graphical elements that determine the essence of spatial order. Potentially, they can establish a visual language system that gives form meaning, purpose, and feeling.

Developing a visual language requires a rigorous examination of how all elements function as a harmonious whole. The properties of a form's visual language define its visual character and visual aesthetic

Envisioning a destination or direction for structuring form comes from a method that enables inventiveness, ignites imagination, and enriches the visual experience. It is a process that begins with an in-depth understanding of the ordinary relationships of the elements and pushing those elements beyond our preconceived expectations. The five components of the process are exploration, experimentation, execution, evaluation, and elevation.

Once a design problem has been defined, the process begins with exploration. Generating multiple ideas from as many different sources as possible stimulates thinking and broadens possibilities— good and bad. From multiple ideas, a few will show promise. Through experimentation, one prominent direction will likely emerge.

Executing the concept and producing the form involves managing the mass/space elements and their variables. In the process of producing the form, image modification and evolution are applied after careful evaluation of the structural elements. Once the analysis is complete, it is important to rework the details that will elevate the form to exquisitely balanced proportions.

The methodology of the five stages of the form development process is fundamental to establishing a visual language and inventiveness.

exploration

experimentation.

execution

EVALUATION

elevation

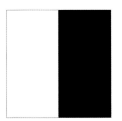 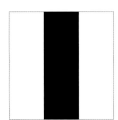

An ordering strategy begins with defining the image area format and a method for activating that space. Applying a square format makes it possible to enact visual observations in an environment where the height and width are mathematically constant. Dividing the space along one of the implied forces within the square establishes directional axis limitations. An examination of the vertical image area axis is an explicit orientation for activating the two-dimensional space of the square. Limiting the visual elements to directional axis and lines/rectangles limits options to number and size. Placing limitations on line, shape, color, size, texture, and position encour-ages exploration and experimentation.

A logical figure–ground sequence of lines/rectangles can form a basic organizational strategy. It is a structural strategy that facilitates the ordering of static and dynamic visual systems.

The first and most obvious ordering system is composed of a regular sequence where the black-and-white parts appear to be uniform in width and length, and equal in size. There is no directional movement and no contrast in size. The figure/ground relationship is ambiguous— neither the black nor white is established as figure or ground. The ordering system is predictably repetitive.

The second system establishes an alternating sequence of visual contrast in the sizes between the black and white. The image remains relatively static with no directional eye movement, and the ordering system is readily apparent. In this image, the smaller part becomes the figure resting on the ground. Spatially, the figure resides in front of the background.

Within the perceived attributes of the mass/space elements there are two variables that can be manipulated. Each variable is dependant upon the other. One variable is size/scale and the other is number. In this example, two rectangles equal in size define the square. Mathematically the image is defined as having three parts—one square and two rectangles. Visually, the image is defined as having two rectangular parts.

In this example, there are not enough parts to define a sequence. Mathematically, it takes a minimum of three parts to communicate a numerical sequence. The same logic may be applied to creating a visual sequence.

Additionally, there are no additional black parts to compare a similarity in size and no white parts to compare similarity in size. Therefore, black cannot be constant to black and white cannot be constant to white in size relationships.

In a regular sequence, the figure–ground relationship is ambiguous. Also note that white expands and black contracts. A slight adjustment in the width of each is necessary to make them appear equal. A regular repetitive sequence creates a static image that is bilaterally symmetrical, with minimal contrast, and no directional movement.

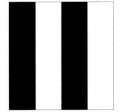 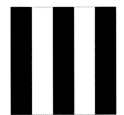 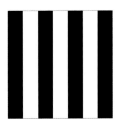 

Likewise, the second image does not conform to a regular ordering sequence. The image defines the square with three rectangles. Once again, there are not enough parts to define a sequence. There are not enough parts of the same color to be sequential. As in the first example, there are no black parts to make a comparison. This arrangement of parts creates a black figure. The two white parts visually group to form a background.

Units of four create black-and-white vertical edges. This image establishes light/dark contrast and a left-to-right visual direction.

A space defined with five units communicates a regular sequence. Although there are only two white units, it may be assumed a regular sequence is in place. Repetition of the three black units establishes a regular pattern. Note that black units are used on the left and right edges of the image area. This helps to contain the sequence within the square, since white tends to expand and black contracts. In addition, black edges are a conventional method used to outline an image.

Employing seven parts is a decisive definition of a regular sequence. There are enough parts in white and black to visually confirm a repetitive pattern.

When the number of white-and-black units increases, a textured field of gray is formed. At this point, the units do not maintain their individual identity to communicate a sequence.

An alternating sequence is composed of units that significantly contrast in size. The width of black parts remains consistent to each other and the width of white parts remains consistent to each other. With extreme contrast in size, an alternating sequence produces a figure that resides on a ground of the opposite color.

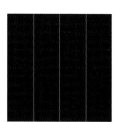

The third system employs successively increasing black units while the white units remain the same size. Since the black parts are sequentially increasing from one side of the square to the other, a directional movement is established. Visual interest is also created through contrast in size. This ordering system has the potential to create a reversal of figure/ground. In a sequence of this type, it is preferable for the parts that are progressively increasing to be more important in the visual hierarchy.

The fourth system is similar to the previous, except the white units are increasing while the black units remain the same in visual appearance.

In the fifth system, both the white parts and the black parts successively increase in size and in the same direction. The sequential ordering of parts is less obvious and predictable. Contrast occurs in size and directional movement is evident. Figure/ground relationships may be incorporated.

The sixth ordering system establishes a successively increasing sequence of black-and-white units moving in opposite directions at different rates while maintaining maximum contrast in size. Given this division of space, the sequential order is generally an underlying structural element. The ordering system in itself is visually less important than the changes in scale and the reversal of figure/ground, but it holds the elements together.

The primary purpose of these organizational strategies is to increase sensitivity to the dual relationship between positive and negative space. Applying restraint, these orderly systems encourage an exploration of contrast, direction, number, repetition, continuity, and variety. Visual sequencing, rhythm, grouping, and similarity are a means of developing compositional harmony. Additionally, objective criteria can be applied for evaluating the strengths and weaknesses of a visual composition.

 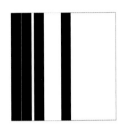 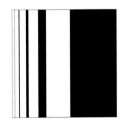 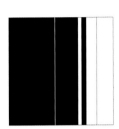

These four examples represent a system of increasing intervals. The first example demonstrates a system with black increasing and white remaining the same in appearance. The second example is similar to the first, but white increases visually. In the fourth example, white and black increase in the same direction. Lastly, white and black increase in opposite directions. Note the figure–ground reversal in these images.

In order to maintain maximum contrast between the white and black units, either white or black must be as small in width dimension as possible. The largest unit must be large enough to permit figure/ground reversal. These images address the Gestalt principle of grouping. If similar color units are close in proximity, the colors will group together and form a field.

Given the scale and proximity of white and black parts, the image area surface suggests movement back into space or causes the surface to appear curved.

The asymmetrical divisions of ordered spatial proportions produce a visually dynamic image. The smallest unit transforming to the largest unit causes a visual direction movement. While the sequence is orderly, it is not visually obvious. Continued visual movement left to right or right to left is dependent upon small parts transforming logically/visually into larger parts. Divisions down the center tend to interrupt the visual transformation.

The proportional relationship between the grouping of black and white units is decisively different. Proportion is a comparison of surface areas.

In a horizontal orientation, the square image area will appear to move back into space when the unit intervals change successively in size. In addition, the square will appear to be a different rectangle, depending on the number of intervals and size contrast.

Depending on the axis orientation, the sixth ordering system will produce different visual characteristics. Horizontal divisions of space are considerably different in appearance when compared to a vertical orientation. The effects alter the size, shape, and space of the square format.

In a horizontal orientation, the image area suggests movement back into space or causes the surface to appear curved. This is caused by the scale and proximity of the diminishing size intervals. This effect is more apparent in the horizontal orientation when compared to other spatial orientations.

The units in these examples are mathematically equal in width dimension. As the lines/shapes get shorter in length, the wider they appear. In an angular orientation, the parallel lines appear to contract along one edge of the square and expand along the horizontal edge of the square.

Diagonal and Angular Interval Systems

The diagonal and angular orientation creates optical effects that make shorter units appear wider than the longer units. Parallel edge relationships appear to expand and contract along edges of the square. It is important to note that a division through the center of the square may interrupt the appearance of increasing/decreasing intervals.

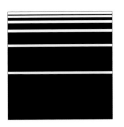  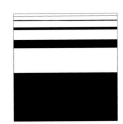 

The basis for developing dynamic visual images resides in

* understanding the principles of two-dimensional organization.

* objective analysis of visual form; fostering visual experiences through exploration, experimentation, and investigation.

* developing a process for organizing a two-dimensional space.

* fundamental compositional properties integrating the mass/space elements and their attributes into a harmonious whole.

That is, all parts must contribute to the development of the image and to the unification of the whole image.

When one ordering system interrupts another, they create shapes or lines depending on scale. A combination of two ordering systems at contrasting angles produces a grid of increasing intervals in two directions. In this example, diagonal axes are employed. The interaction of the two axes produces a right angle relationship of parts. An ordering system of increasing units moving in the same direction interacts with an ordering system of increasing units moving in opposite directions. An organization of line and shape is built along the axis of the two ordering systems.

An evaluation of this compositional arrangement demonstrates contrast in scale, shape, and black-to-white proportional relationships. The composition also incorporates figure/ground reversal. In the color iteration, a split complementary color scheme is employed. All components in the composition are generated by the interaction of the two ordering systems.

Strong compositions tend to have several basic characteristics. There should be contrast in size, decisive changes in white and black, and figure/ground reversal. The concept of closure is also important to dynamic compositions. Closure links different parts together by utilizing proximity and grouping and forces the eye to travel as it connects the parts.

Design: Hannah Lee

 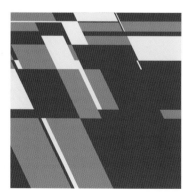

The rectangular format for this composition is defined by the Fibonacci series. Each unit in the series is expressed in an ordering system of white and black intervals increasing in opposite directions.

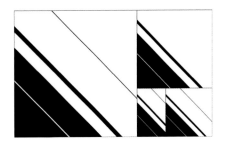

The first three examples demonstrate edited stages of composition development.

The Fibonacci proportional system is implied and maintains its identity in each step of development. The final image employs one dominant axis within the area of the proportional system.

Alignments and trajectories of points and lines assist the eye to connect the parts forming a unified composition. This example integrates the inherent implied dynamics of the proportional system—diagonals, angles, and curves. A primary color harmony is applied to the black-and-white composition.

Design: Mark Grote

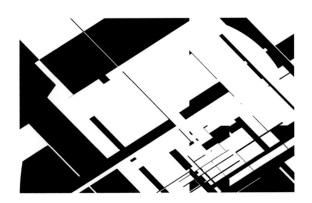

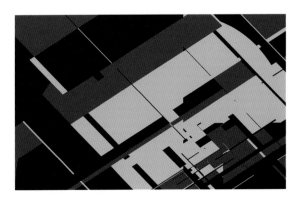

Applied Ordering Strategies

Building a consistent visual language validates a compositional "family of form." In the process of establishing a family of form, there are many organizational methods that may be considered. These methods are all fundamentally integral to the variable relationships of the mass/space elements. Ultimately, visual elements play a critical role in the development of an organizational strategy.

Form elements and attributes are the syntax of the visual language. The syntax defines the patterns of formation among the visual parts. It represents a system of orderly arrangement. Basically, words and images have equal importance, since the images represent the words. Whatever the strategy, all systems employ restraint, intent, and meaning.

Design: Anna Grote

Based upon the whimsical phrase "The Jesus Lizard frantically outruns the sharks," a compositional study of point, line, plane, and shape intervals communicates the intent of the message. Breaking down the line, shape, and text elements into an orderly system, this nine-step storyboard animates the two-dimensional components for a motion piece executed in time-based media.

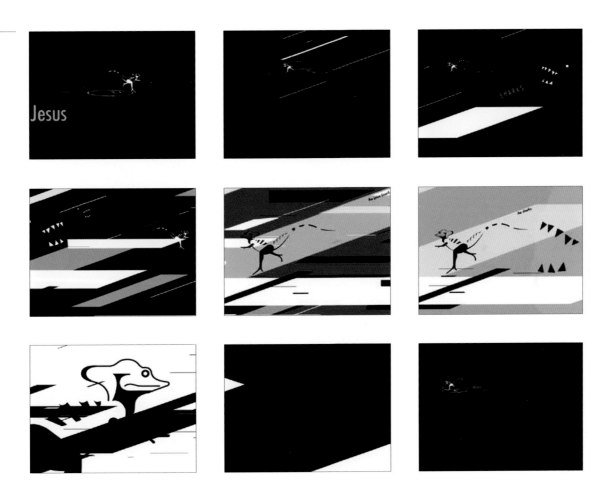

Design: Lindsey N. Meyer

These nine images create a family of form as they incorporate similar visual elements. All nine images are confined within a circle. They are formulated by consistency of line, texture, and visual weight. These images are a representation of natural symbols found in Japanese culture.

The animals in this system represent endangered species of
Australia. The system relies on the similarity of line and shape
through the visual effect of closure.

Design: Jenny Slife

Design: Lisa Bambach

From a collection of the Taft Museum of Art, a set of drawings identifies time, places, and artifacts of art, architecture, and design. This system shares a commonality of a line, which serves as a base anchor. Line weights, geometry, closure, and proportions provide consistency without sacrificing object identity and meaning.

These drawings are a collection of scientific instruments based on historical significance. The drawings demonstrate a visually cohesive character suitable to its identity and purpose. Circular shapes, line weights, and light/dark relationships define the family of form. In addition, the geometry of the form is indicative of the mechanical function of the object.

Design: Anna Grote

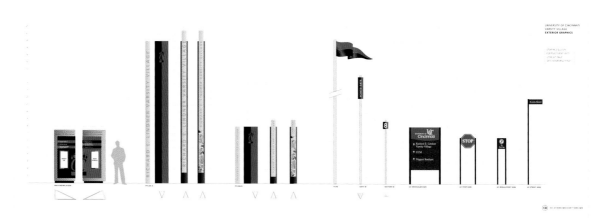

Using shapes and lines derived from the pathways concept creates the essence of the visual system. Shapes can be made into lines and color bars and layered to create depths. Elements can be subtracted to enhance the design. The possibilities are endless. Because they derive from the same system, line and shape patterns create a consistent link and identity for visual communication at the University of Cincinnati.

As shown in these examples, interior and exterior environmental signage conforms to identity standards. The same organizational strategy is applied to all forms of visual communication.

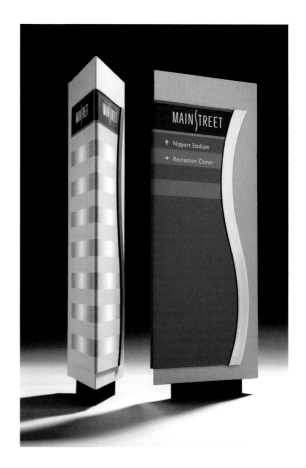

Design: Kolar Design

149

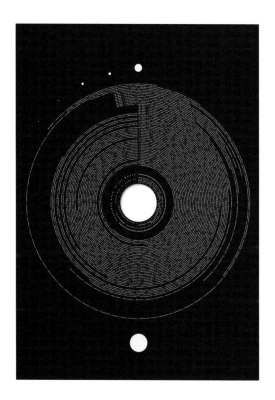

A system of dots and concentric circles is used in these information graphics posters. "Everyone Ever in the World" is a visual representation of the number of people to have lived versus those who have lost their lives in wars, massacres, and genocide throughout recorded history. The visualization uses existing paper area and die cuts to represent the concepts of life and death.

The graph exemplifies the value imparted to data with regard to the manner in which it is visualized. The relative simplicity and graphical approach affords the viewer an instantaneous assessment of the degree to which conflict has shaped human history.

The organizational strategy demonstrates simplicity of visual representation that imparts a somber and respectful tone to such a weighty subject.

Design: Peter Crnokrak

strategic
COMPLIANCE

planning for success

We begin every project by listening to you and surveying the competitive landscape. We
gather data, analyze for trends, weigh options. Our unbiased thinking provides you with a fresh
perspective on your business and your challenges. Then we use that insight and information to
develop guidelines that inform the creative process and measure the success of every project.

To ensure that you *reap the benefits* of our lean structure, we augment
our team with marketing professionals with the skills that enable us to craft
a comprehensive, cost-effective communication strategy.

In this promotional brochure, visual metaphors
illustrate the characteristics of the company's
process—the drafted quality of compliance, the
pulsing emanation of creativity, and the tar-
geted precision of consistency. Each illustration
capitalizes on a circular form and uses a radial
grid in both simple and complex ways. Color
harmonies of similarly saturated colors are
based on various fundamental structural triads.

The layout of the piece depends on a strong
horizontal band that leads the eye through the
piece. Fold-out pages conceal and reveal multiple levels of information.

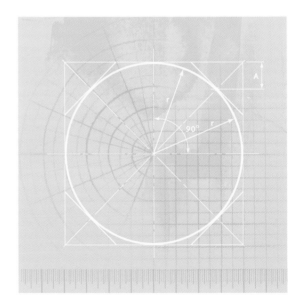

implementing
CONSISTENCY

synergy and unity

We work to ensure that every dollar spent is an investment in elevating your brand. By developing comprehensive brand standards, we give you a system that not only helps ensure consistent communication to your stakeholders but also prevents inconsistencies that erode brand image and value.

evolving
CREATIVITY

a process for inspired creative

Our design team uses experience and employs a proven design methodology refined through years of partnering with some of the world's largest and most valuable corporate brands. While many designers start their work on the computer, we choose to begin by exploring collaboratively, sketching by hand to quickly capture flashes of inspiration. We feel this results in stronger creative results and is the best way to inspire communications that are both effective and unexpected. Our goal is to design creative solutions that serve as a catalyst for your company's growth.

Design: Madison Design Group

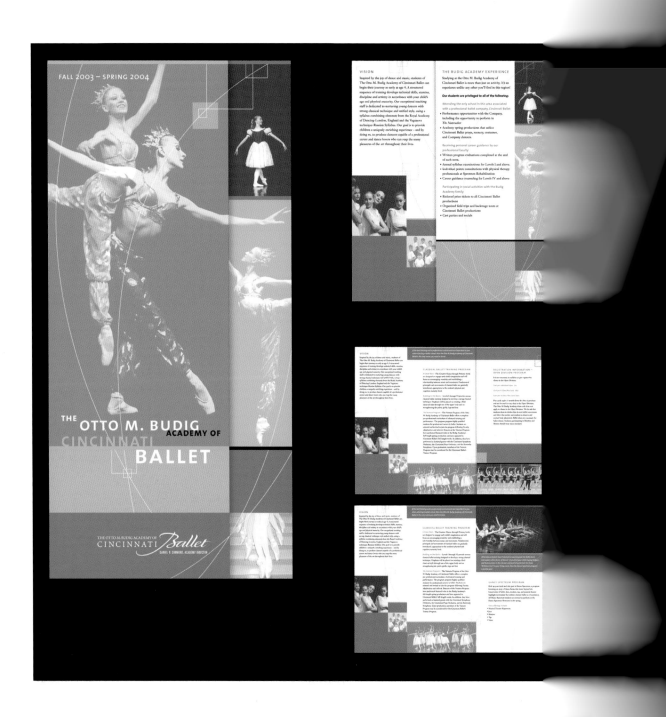

This system created for the Cincinnati Ballet blends refined geometric and poetic forms. The concept is also based upon paradoxical wordplay—current yet time-less, elegant yet bold, sophisticated yet accessible.

Design: Stanard Desi

STATUE OF LIBERTY

ELLIS ISLAND

GOVERNORS ISLAND

LOWER EAST SIDE TENEMENT MUSEUM

FEDERAL HALL

CASTLE CLINTON

GENERAL GRANT ★★★ MEMORIAL

ST. PAUL'S CHURCH

HAMILTON GRANGE

THEODORE ROOSEVELT BIRTHPLACE

GATEWAY

FORT WADSWORTH

MILLER FIELD

GREAT KILLS PARK

CANARSIE PIER

SANDY HOOK

FORT HANCOCK

JAMAICA BAY

FLOYD BENNETT FIELD

FORT TILDEN

JACOB RIIS PARK

BREEZY POINT

In an effort to build public awareness, a distinctive identity program was created for the National Parks of New York Harbor. The goal was to develop a memorable graphic system to identify the family of sites, while also allowing each location its own unique image. Ultimately, twenty-three separate "wordmarks" were created from a whimsical, changing alphabet inspired by the specific features of each place.

Design: Steff Geissbuhler
C&G Partners

155

"Graphic design—
    which fulfils aesthetic needs,
    complies with the laws of form
    and the exigencies of two-dimensional space;
    which speaks in semiotics, sans-serifs,
    and geometries;
    which abstracts, transforms, translates,
    rotates, dilates, repeats, mirrors,
    groups, and regroups—
    is not good design
    if it is irrelevant."

"Graphic design—
    which evokes the symmetria of Vitruvius,
    the dynamic symmetry of Hambidge,
    the asymmetry of Mondrian;
    which is a good gestalt;
    which is generated by intuition or by
    computer,
    by invention or by a system or coordinates—
    is not good design
    if it does not co-operate
    as an instrument
    in the service of communication."

—Paul Rand

So this is where order and structure facilitate restraint. It is where thoughtful application of the elements fosters visual aptitude. Where understanding and meaning are embedded in context and content. It is the place where form and communication coexist in visual harmony. It is the place where creativity is ignited.

the language of form

ELEMENTS	ATTRIBUTES	PERCEPTIONS
		hierarchy
		alignment, position, projection, trajectory, orientation, direction, proximity, rotation
		sequence/interval
		transitions, connections, convergence, terminations
		number/density
		axis
POINT	COLOR	balance
LINE	SIZE	symmetry
PLANE	SHAPE	tension
VOLUME	TEXTURE	rhythm
		closure
		fluctuation
		afterimage
		grouping
		focal point

index

a–c

d–g

m–p

Design Elements: Form & Space

p–s

t–w

contributors

AIGA Symbol Sign Commission
60 · 61

Lisa Bambach
104 · 126 · 146

Michael Bierut
Pentagram Design
www.pentagram.com
48 · 73

Michael Bierut
Armin Vit
Pentagram Design
31

Michael Bierut
Jennifer Kinon
Pentagram Design
42

Michael Bierut
Joe Marianek
Pentagram Design
67

Michael Bierut
Yve Ludwig
Pentagram Design
107

Yulia Brodskaya
United Kingdom
www.artyulia.com
70 · 71

Christina Cahalene
www.christinacahalane.com
68

Karen Cheng
Seattle, WA
www.cheng-design.com
125

Chermayeff & Geismar
137 East 25th Street
New York, NY 10010
www.cgstudionyc.com
50 · 51 · 52 · 53 · 58 · 64 · 65 · 106

Peter Crnokrak
London, U.K.
150 · 151

Kristin Cullen
www.kristincullen.com
30 · 36 · 37 · 39 · 48 · 58 · 126 · 127

Branden Francis
46

Laura Frycek
38 · 41 · 78 · 91 · 105 · 126

Steff Geisbuhler
C&G Partners
116 East 16 Street
New York, NY 10003
www.cgpartnersllc.com
59 · 79 · 107 · 155

Anna Grote
142 · 143 · 147

Mark Grote
105 · 141

Joseph Howell
78

Darrin Hunter
www.dishdesign.com
21 · 105

Victoria Karoleff
18 · 37

Kolar Design, Inc.
660 Lincoln Avenue
Cincinnati, OH 45206,
www.kolardesign.net
Bernard Tschumi Architects,
Eva Maddox, glaserworks,
Hargreaves Associates
Marcia Shortt Design
148 · 149

Lucas Langus
18 · 20 · 78

Acknowledgments

Writing and designing a book requires commitment and determination. It also requires the enlightenment, vision, and wisdom of numerous individuals. I wish to extend heartfelt gratitude to those who assisted and encouraged me along the way.

Rockport Publishers, Betsy Gammons, Emily Potts, and Regina Grenier—for their advice, guidance, and patience

My students—for their enthusiasm and creativity

Colleagues at the University of Cincinnati and North Carolina State University—for stimulating intellectual curiosity

Kristin Cullen—for her generosity and astute observations, a friend and colleague

Melissa and Kurt, Matthew and Aliy—for their insight, encouragement, and unwavering loyalty

Diana—for her trust, faith, and words of wisdom

Finally, I wish to dedicate this book to my guardian angels, Lilly and Mia—my source of inspiration and motivation.

About the Author

Dennis Puhalla is professor of design at the University of Cincinnati, College of Design, Architecture, Art, and Planning. He teaches undergraduate and graduate courses in visual language design, motion design, color theory, and principles of two- and three-dimensional design. Students and colleagues recognize him for his outstanding teaching. Professor Puhalla served as director of the School of Design for ten years, initiating innovative and visionary programs. He earned a doctorate in design from North Carolina State University, College of Design. He holds a master of fine arts and a bachelor of science in design from the University of Cincinnati, College of Design, Architecture, Art, and Planning.

Puhalla's professional work has been exhibited nationally and is included in public and private collections. Puhalla is committed to the field of design as a practitioner and consultant.